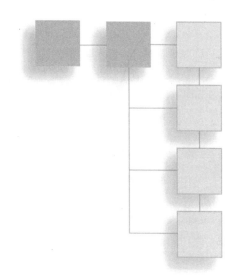

PYTHON®
PROGRAMMING
FOR TEENS

WITHDRAWN

KENNETH A. LAMBERT

Cengage Learning PTR

Professional • Technical • Reference

Australia • Brazil • Japan • Korea • Mexico • Singapore • Spain • United Kingdom • United States

CENGAGE
Learning

Professional • Technical • Reference

Python® Programming for Teens
Kenneth A. Lambert

Publisher and General Manager,
Cengage Learning PTR: Stacy L. Hiquet

Associate Director of Marketing:
Sarah Panella

Manager of Editorial Services:
Heather Talbot

Senior Marketing Manager:
Mark Hughes

Senior Product Manager: Mitzi Koontz

Project/Copy Editor: Karen A. Gill

Technical Reviewer: Zach Scott

Interior Layout Tech: MPS Limited

Cover Designer: Mike Tanamachi

Indexer: Sharon Shock

Proofreader: Gene Redding

For product information and technology assistance, contact us at **Cengage Learning Customer & Sales Support, 1-800-354-9706**.

For permission to use material from this text or product, submit all requests online at **cengage.com/permissions**.

Further permissions questions can be emailed to **permissionrequest@cengage.com**.

Python is a registered trademark of the Python Software Foundation.

All other trademarks are the property of their respective owners.

All images © Cengage Learning unless otherwise noted.

Library of Congress Control Number: 2014939193

ISBN-13: 978-1-305-27195-1

ISBN-10: 1-305-27195-5

Cengage Learning PTR

20 Channel Center Street

Boston, MA 02210

USA

Cengage Learning is a leading provider of customized learning solutions with office locations around the globe, including Singapore, the United Kingdom, Australia, Mexico, Brazil, and Japan. Locate your local office at: **international.cengage.com/region**.

Cengage Learning products are represented in Canada by Nelson Education, Ltd.

For your lifelong learning solutions, visit **cengageptr.com**.

Visit our corporate website at **cengage.com**.

Printed in the United States of America
1 2 3 4 5 6 7 16 15 14

To my wife Carolyn, with much gratitude.
Kenneth A. Lambert
Lexington, Virginia

Acknowledgments

I would like to thank my friend Martin Osborne for many years of advice, friendly criticism, and encouragement on several of my book projects.

I would also like to thank Zach Scott, MQA Tester, who helped to ensure that the content of all data and solution files used for this text were correct and accurate; Karen Gill, my project editor and copy editor; and Mitzi Koontz, senior product manager at Cengage Learning PTR.

ABOUT THE AUTHOR

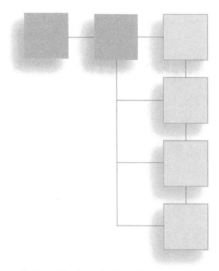

Kenneth A. Lambert is a professor of computer science and the chair of that department at Washington and Lee University. He has taught introductory programming courses for 29 years and has been an active researcher in computer science education. Lambert has authored or coauthored 25 textbooks, including a series of introductory C++ textbooks with Douglas Nance and Thomas Naps, a series of introductory Java textbooks with Martin Osborne, and a series of introductory Python textbooks. His most recent textbook is *Fundamentals of Python: Data Structures*.

Contents

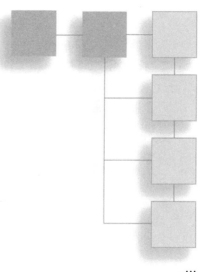

Chapter 2   **Getting Started with Turtle Graphics** **31**

Chapter 3   **Control Structures: Sequencing, Iteration, and Selection** **55**

INTRODUCTION

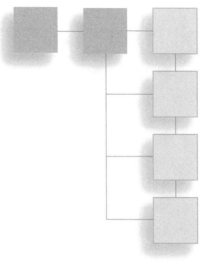

Welcome to *Python Programming for Teens*. Whether you're under 20 or just a teenager at heart, this book will introduce you to computer programming. You can use it in a classroom or on your own. The only assumption is that you know how to use a modern computer system with a keyboard, screen, and mouse.

To make your learning experience fun and interesting, you will write programs that draw pictures on the screen and allow you to interact with them by using the mouse. Along the way, you will learn the basic principles of program design and problem solving with computers. You will then be able to apply these ideas and techniques to solve problems in almost any area of study. But most of all, you will experience the joy of building things that work *and* look great!

WHY PYTHON?

Computer technology and applications have become increasingly more sophisticated over the past several decades, and so has the computer science curriculum, especially at the introductory level. Today's students learn a bit of programming and problem solving and are then expected to move quickly into topics like software development, complexity analysis, and data structures that, 20 years ago, were reserved for advanced courses. In addition, the ascent of object-oriented programming as a dominant method has led instructors and textbook authors to bring powerful, industrial-strength programming languages such as C++ and Java into the introductory curriculum. As a result, instead of experiencing the rewards and excitement of computer programming, beginning students often become overwhelmed by the combined tasks of mastering advanced concepts and learning the syntax of a programming language.

This book uses the Python programming language as a way of making the learning experience manageable and attractive for students and instructors alike. Python offers the following pedagogical benefits:

- Python has simple, conventional syntax. Its statements are close to those of ordinary English, and its expressions use the conventional notation found in algebra. Thus, beginners can spend less time learning the syntax of a programming language and more time learning to solve interesting problems.

- Python has safe semantics. Any expression or statement whose meaning violates the definition of the language produces an error message.

- Python scales well. It is easy for beginners to write simple programs. Python also includes all the advanced features of a modern programming language, such as support for data structures and object-oriented software development, for use when they become necessary.

- Python is highly interactive. Expressions and statements can be entered at an interpreter's prompts to allow the programmer to try out experimental code and receive immediate feedback. Longer code segments can then be composed and saved in script files to be loaded and run as modules or standalone applications.

- Python is general purpose. In today's context, this means that the language includes resources for contemporary applications, including media computing and networks.

- Python is free and is in widespread use in the industry. Students can download it to run on a variety of devices. There is a large Python user community, and expertise in Python programming has great resume value.

To summarize these benefits, Python is a comfortable and flexible vehicle for expressing ideas about computation, both for beginners and experts alike. If students learn these ideas well in their first experience with programming, they should have no problems making a quick transition to other languages and technologies needed to achieve their educational or career objectives. Most importantly, beginners will spend less time staring at a computer screen and more time thinking about interesting problems to solve.

ORGANIZATION OF THE BOOK

The approach in this book is easygoing, with each new concept introduced only when you need it.

Chapter 1, "Getting Started with Python," advises you how to download, install, and start the Python programming software used in this book. You try out simple program commands and become acquainted with the basic features of the Python language that you will use throughout the book.

Chapter 2, "Getting Started with Turtle Graphics," introduces the basic commands for turtle graphics. You learn to draw pictures with a set of simple commands. Along the way, you discover a thing or two about colors and two-dimensional geometry.

Chapter 3, "Control Structures: Sequencing, Iteration, and Selection," covers the program commands that allow the computer to make choices and perform repetitive tasks.

Chapters 4, "Composing, Saving, and Running Programs," shows you how to save your programs in files, so you can give them to others or work on them another day. You learn how to organize a program like an essay, so it is easy for you and others to read, understand, and edit. You also learn a bit about how the computer is able to read, understand, and run a program.

Chapter 5, "Defining Functions," introduces an important design feature: the function. By organizing your programs with functions, you can simplify complex tasks and eliminate unnecessary duplications in your code.

Chapter 6, "User Interaction with the Mouse and the Keyboard," covers features that allow people to interact with your programs. You learn program commands for responding to mouse and keyboard events, as well as pop-up dialogs that can take information from your programs' users.

Chapter 7, "Recursion," teaches you about another important design strategy called recursion. You write some recursive functions that generate computer art and fractal images.

Chapter 8, "Objects and Classes," offers a beginner's guide to the use of objects and classes in programming. You learn how to define new types of objects, such as menu items for choosing colors and grids for board games, and use them in interesting programs.

Chapter 9, "Animations," concludes the book with a brief introduction to animations. You discover how to get images to move independently and interact in interesting ways.

Two appendixes follow the last chapter. Appendix A, "Turtle Graphics Commands," provides a reference for the set of turtle graphics commands introduced in the book.

Each chapter includes a set of two programming exercises that build on concepts and examples introduced earlier in that chapter. You can find the answers to these exercises in Appendix B, "Solutions to Exercises."

COMPANION WEBSITE DOWNLOADS

You may download the companion website files from www.cengageptr.com/downloads. These files include the example programs discussed in the book and the solutions to the exercises.

A BRIEF HISTORY OF COMPUTING

Before you jump ahead to programming, you might want to peek at some context. The following table summarizes some of the major developments in the history of computing. The discussion that follows provides more details about these developments.

Approximate Date	Major Developments
Before 1800	Mathematicians develop and use algorithms Abacus used as a calculating aide First mechanical calculators built by Leibniz and Pascal
1800–1930	Jacquard's loom Babbage's Analytical Engine Boole's system of logic Hollerith's punch card machine
1930s	Turing publishes results on computability Shannon's theory of information and digital switching
1940s	First electronic digital computers
1950s	First symbolic programming languages Transistors make computers smaller, faster, more durable, less expensive Emergence of data-processing applications
1960–1975	Integrated circuits accelerate the miniaturization of computer hardware First minicomputers Time-sharing operating systems Interactive user interfaces with keyboards and monitors Proliferation of high-level programming languages Emergence of a software industry and the academic study of computer science and computer engineering

1975–1990	First microcomputers and mass-produced personal computers
	Graphical user interfaces become widespread
	Networks and the Internet
1990–2000	Optical storage (CDs, DVDs)
	Laptop computers
	Multimedia applications (music, photography, video)
	Computer-assisted manufacturing, retail, and finance
	World Wide Web and e-commerce
2000–present	Embedded computing (cars, appliances, and so on)
	Handheld music and video players
	Smartphones and tablets
	Touch screen user interfaces
	Wireless and cloud computing
	Search engines
	Social networks

Before Electronic Digital Computers

The term *algorithm*, as it's now used, refers to a recipe or method for solving a problem. It consists of a sequence of well-defined instructions or steps that describe a process that halts with a solution to a problem.

Ancient mathematicians developed the first algorithms. The word "algorithm" comes from the name of a Persian mathematician, Muhammad ibn Musa Al-Khawarizmi, who wrote several mathematics textbooks in the ninth century. About 2,300 years ago, the Greek mathematician Euclid, the inventor of geometry, developed an algorithm for computing the greatest common divisor of two numbers, which you will see later in this book.

A device known as the *abacus* also appeared in ancient times to help people perform simple arithmetic. Users calculated sums and differences by sliding beads on a grid of wires. The configuration of beads on the abacus served as the data.

In the seventeenth century, the French mathematician Blaise Pascal (1623–1662) built one of the first mechanical devices to automate the process of addition. The addition operation was embedded in the configuration of gears within the machine. The user entered the two numbers to be added by rotating some wheels. The sum or output number then appeared on another rotating wheel. The German mathematician Gottfried Leibnitz

(1646–1716) built another mechanical calculator that included other arithmetic functions such as multiplication. Leibnitz, who with Newton also invented calculus, went on to propose the idea of computing with symbols as one of our most basic and general intellectual activities. He argued for a universal language in which one could solve any problem by calculating.

Early in the nineteenth century, the French engineer Joseph Jacquard (1752–1834) designed and constructed a machine that automated the process of weaving. Until then, each row in a weaving pattern had to be set up by hand, a quite tedious, error-prone process. Jacquard's loom was designed to accept input in the form of a set of punched cards. Each card described a row in a pattern of cloth. Although it was still an entirely mechanical device, Jacquard's loom possessed something that previous devices had lacked—the ability to carry out the instructions of an algorithm automatically. The set of cards expressed the algorithm or set of instructions that controlled the behavior of the loom. If the loom operator wanted to produce a different pattern, he just had to run the machine with a different set of cards.

The British mathematician Charles Babbage (1792–1871) took the concept of a programmable computer a step further by designing a model of a machine that, conceptually, bore a striking resemblance to a modern general-purpose computer. Babbage conceived his machine, which he called the Analytical Engine, as a mechanical device. His design called for four functional parts: a mill to perform arithmetic operations, a store to hold data and a program, an operator to run the instructions from punched cards, and an output to produce the results on punched cards. Sadly, Babbage's computer was never built. The project perished for lack of funds near the time when Babbage himself passed away.

In the last two decades of the nineteenth century, a U.S. Census Bureau statistician named Herman Hollerith (1860–1929) developed a machine that automated data processing for the U.S. Census. Hollerith's machine, which had the same component parts as Babbage's Analytical Engine, simply accepted a set of punched cards as input and then tallied and sorted the cards. His machine greatly shortened the time it took to produce statistical results on the U.S. population. Government and business organizations seeking to automate their data processing quickly adopted Hollerith's punched card machines. Hollerith was also one of the founders of a company that eventually became IBM (International Business Machines).

Also in the nineteenth century, the British secondary school teacher George Boole (1815–1864) developed a system of logic. This system consisted of a pair of values, TRUE and FALSE, and a set of three primitive operations on these values, AND, OR, and NOT. Boolean logic eventually became the basis for designing the electronic circuitry to process binary information.

A half a century later, in the 1930s, the British mathematician Alan Turing (1912–1954) explored the theoretical foundations and limits of algorithms and computation. Turing's most important contributions were to develop the concept of a universal machine that could be specialized to solve any computable problems and to demonstrate that some problems are unsolvable by computers.

The First Electronic Digital Computers (1940–1950)

In the late 1930s, Claude Shannon (1916–2001), a mathematician and electrical engineer at MIT, wrote a classic paper titled "A Symbolic Analysis of Relay and Switching Circuits." In this paper, he showed how operations and information in other systems, such as arithmetic, could be reduced to Boolean logic and then to hardware. For example, if the Boolean values TRUE and FALSE were written as the binary digits 1 and 0, one could write a sequence of logical operations to compute the sum of two strings of binary digits. All that was required to build an electronic digital computer was the ability to represent binary digits as on/off switches and to represent the logical operations in other circuitry.

The needs of the combatants in World War II pushed the development of computer hardware into high gear. Several teams of scientists and engineers in the United States, Great Britain, and Germany independently created the first generation of general-purpose digital electronic computers during the 1940s. All these scientists and engineers used Shannon's innovation of expressing binary digits and logical operations in terms of electronic switching devices. Among these groups was a team at Harvard University under the direction of Howard Aiken. Their computer, called the Mark I, became operational in 1944 and did mathematical work for the U.S. Navy during the war. The Mark I was considered an electromechanical device because it used a combination of magnets, relays, and gears to store and process data.

Another team under J. Presper Eckert and John Mauchly, at the University of Pennsylvania, produced a computer called the ENIAC (Electronic Numerical Integrator and Calculator). The ENIAC calculated ballistics tables for the artillery of the U.S. Army toward the end of the war. Because the ENIAC used entirely electronic components, it was almost a thousand times faster than the Mark I.

Two other electronic digital computers were completed a bit earlier than the ENIAC. They were the ABC (Atanasoff-Berry Computer), built by John Atanasoff and Clifford

Berry at Iowa State University in 1942, and the Colossus, constructed by a group working with Alan Turing in England in 1943. The ABC was created to solve systems of simultaneous linear equations. Although the ABC's function was much narrower than that of the ENIAC, the ABC is now regarded as the first electronic digital computer. The Colossus, whose existence had been top secret until recently, was used to crack the powerful German Enigma code during the war.

The first electronic digital computers, sometimes called *mainframe computers*, consisted of vacuum tubes, wires, and plugs, and they filled entire rooms. Although they were much faster than people at computing, by our own current standards they were extraordinarily slow and prone to breakdown. Moreover, the early computers were extremely difficult to program. To enter or modify a program, a team of workers had to rearrange the connections among the vacuum tubes by unplugging and replugging the wires. Each program was loaded by literally hardwiring it into the computer. With thousands of wires involved, it was easy to make a mistake.

The memory of these first computers stored only data, not the program that processed the data. As you have read, the idea of a stored program first appeared 100 years earlier in Jacquard's loom and in Babbage's design for the Analytical Engine. In 1946, John von Neumann realized that the instructions of the programs could also be stored in binary form in an electronic digital computer's memory. His research group at Princeton developed one of the first modern stored-program computers.

Although the size, speed, and applications of computers have changed dramatically since those early days, the basic architecture and design of the electronic digital computer have remained remarkably stable.

The First Programming Languages (1950–1965)

The typical computer user now runs many programs, made up of millions of lines of code, that perform what would have seemed like magical tasks 20 or 30 years ago. But the first digital electronic computers had no software as today's do. The machine code for a few relatively simple and small applications had to be loaded by hand. As the demand for larger and more complex applications grew, so did the need for tools to expedite the programming process.

In the early 1950s, computer scientists realized that a symbolic notation could be used instead of machine code, and the first *assembly languages* appeared. The programmers would enter mnemonic codes for operations, such as ADD and OUTPUT, and for data variables, such as SALARY and RATE, at a *keypunch machine*. The keystrokes punched a set of holes in a small card for each instruction. The programmers then carried their stacks of cards to a system operator, who placed them in a device called a *card reader*. This device translated the holes in the cards to patterns in the computer's memory. A program called an *assembler* then translated the application programs in memory to machine code and executed them.

Programming in assembly language was a definite improvement over programming in machine code. The symbolic notation used in assembly languages was easier for people to read and understand. Another advantage was that the assembler could catch some programming errors before the program actually executed. However, the symbolic notation still appeared a bit arcane compared to the notations of conventional mathematics. To remedy this problem, John Backus, a programmer working for IBM, developed FORTRAN (Formula Translation Language) in 1954. Programmers, many of whom were mathematicians, scientists, and engineers, could now use conventional algebraic notation. FORTRAN programmers still entered their programs on a keypunch machine, but the computer executed them after a *compiler* translated them to machine code.

FORTRAN was considered ideal for numerical and scientific applications. However, expressing the kind of data used in data processing—in particular, textual information—was difficult. For example, FORTRAN was not practical for processing information that included people's names, addresses, Social Security numbers, and the financial data of corporations and other institutions. In the early 1960s, a team led by Rear Admiral Grace Murray Hopper developed COBOL (Common Business Oriented Language) for data processing in the United States government. Banks, insurance companies, and other institutions were quick to adopt its use in data-processing applications.

Also in the late 1950s and early 1960s, John McCarthy, a computer scientist at MIT, developed a powerful and elegant notation called LISP (List Processing) for expressing computations. Based on a theory of recursive functions (a subject covered in Chapter 7 of this book), LISP captured the essence of symbolic information processing. A student of McCarthy's, Stephen "Slug" Russell, coded the first *interpreter* for LISP in 1960. The interpreter accepted LISP expressions directly as inputs, evaluated them, and printed their results. In its early days, LISP was used primarily for laboratory experiments in an area of research known as *artificial intelligence*. More recently, LISP has been touted as an ideal language for solving any difficult or complex problems.

Although they were among the first high-level programming languages, FORTAN and LISP have survived for decades. They have undergone many modifications to improve their capabilities and have served as models for the development of many other programming languages. COBOL, by contrast, is no longer in active use but has survived mainly in the form of legacy programs that must still be maintained.

These new, high-level programming languages had one feature in common: *abstraction*. In science or any other area of enquiry, an abstraction allows human beings to reduce complex ideas or entities to simpler ones. For example, a set of ten assembly language instructions might be replaced with an equivalent algebraic expression that consists of only five symbols in FORTRAN. Put another way, any time you can say more with less, you are using an abstraction. The use of abstraction is also found in other areas of computing, such as hardware design and information architecture. The complexities don't actually go away, but the abstractions hide them from view. The suppression of distracting complexity with abstractions allows computer scientists to conceptualize, design, and build ever more sophisticated and complex systems.

Integrated Circuits, Interaction, and Timesharing (1965–1975)

In the late 1950s, the vacuum tube gave way to the *transistor* as the mechanism for implementing the electronic switches in computer hardware. As a *solid-state device*, the transistor was much smaller, more reliable, more durable, and less expensive to manufacture than a vacuum tube. Consequently, the hardware components of computers generally became smaller in physical size, more reliable, and less expensive. The smaller and more numerous the switches became, the faster the processing and the greater the capacity of memory to store information.

The development of the *integrated circuit* in the early 1960s allowed computer engineers to build ever smaller, faster, and less expensive computer hardware components. They perfected a process of photographically etching transistors and other solid-state components onto thin wafers of silicon, leaving an entire processor and memory on a single chip. In 1965, Gordon Moore, one of the founders of the computer chip manufacturer Intel, made a prediction that came to be known as *Moore's Law*. This prediction states that the processing speed and storage capacity of hardware will increase and its cost will decrease by approximately a factor of 2 every 18 months. This trend has held true for the past 50 years. For example, there were about 50 electrical components on a chip in 1965, whereas by 2010, a chip could hold more than 60 million components. Without the integrated circuit, men would not have gone to the moon in 1969, and the world would be without the powerful and inexpensive handheld devices that people now use on a daily basis.

Minicomputers the size of a large office desk appeared in the 1960s. The means of developing and running programs were changing. Until then, a computer was typically located in a restricted area with a single human operator. Programmers composed their programs on keypunch machines in another room or building. They then delivered their stacks of cards to the computer operator, who loaded them into a card reader and compiled and ran the programs in sequence on the computer. Programmers then returned to pick up the output results, in the form of new stacks of cards or printouts. This mode of operation, also called *batch processing*, might cause a programmer to wait days for results, including error messages.

The increases in processing speed and memory capacity enabled computer scientists to develop the first *time-sharing operating system*. John McCarthy, the creator of the programming language LISP, recognized that a program could automate many of the functions performed by the human system operator. When memory, including magnetic secondary storage, became large enough to hold several users' programs at the same time, the programs could be scheduled for *concurrent processing*. Each process associated with a program would run for a slice of time and then yield the CPU to another process. All the active processes would repeatedly cycle for a turn with the CPU until they finished.

Several users could now run their own programs simultaneously by entering commands at separate terminals connected to a single computer. As processor speeds continued to increase, each user gained the illusion that a time-sharing computer system belonged entirely to him.

By the late 1960s, programmers could enter program input at a terminal and see program output immediately displayed on a *CRT (Cathode Ray Tube) screen*. Compared to its predecessors, this new computer system was both highly interactive and much more accessible to its users.

Many relatively small and medium-sized institutions, such as universities, were now able to afford computers. These machines were used not only for data processing and engineering applications, but for teaching and research in the new and rapidly growing field of computer science.

Personal Computing and Networks (1975–1990)

In the mid-1960s, Douglas Engelbart, a computer scientist working at the Stanford Research Institute (SRI), first saw one of the ultimate implications of Moore's Law: eventually, perhaps within a generation, hardware components would become small enough and affordable enough to mass produce an individual computer for every human being. What form would these personal computers take, and how would their owners use them? Two decades earlier, in 1945, Engelbart had read an article in *The Atlantic Monthly* titled "As We May Think" that had already posed this question and offered some answers. The author, Vannevar Bush, a scientist at MIT, predicted that computing devices would serve as repositories of information, and ultimately, of all human knowledge. Owners of computing devices would consult this information by browsing through it with pointing devices and contribute information to the knowledge base almost at will. Engelbart agreed that the primary purpose of the personal computer would be to augment the human intellect, and he spent the rest of his career designing computer systems that would accomplish this goal.

During the late 1960s, Engelbart built the first pointing device, or mouse. He also designed software to represent windows, icons, and pull-down menus on a *bit-mapped display screen*. He demonstrated that a computer user could not only enter text at the keyboard but directly manipulate the icons that represent files, folders, and computer applications on the screen.

But for Engelbart, personal computing did not mean computing in isolation. He participated in the first experiment to connect computers in a network, and he believed that soon people would use computers to communicate, share information, and collaborate on team projects.

Engelbart developed his first experimental system, which he called NLS (oNLine System) Augment, on a minicomputer at SRI. In the early 1970s, he moved to Xerox PARC (Palo Alto Research Center) and worked with a team under Alan Kay to develop the first desktop computer system. Called the Alto, this system had many of the features of Engelbart's Augment, as well as email and a functioning hypertext (a forerunner of the World Wide Web). Kay's group also developed a programming language called Smalltalk, which was designed to create programs for the new computer and to teach programming to children. Kay's goal was to develop a personal computer the size of a large notebook, which he called the Dynabook. Unfortunately for Xerox, the company's management had more interest in photocopy machines than in the work of Kay's visionary research group. However, a young entrepreneur named Steve Jobs visited the Xerox lab and saw the Alto in action. In 1984, Apple Computer, the now-famous company founded by Steve Jobs, brought forth the Macintosh, the first successful mass-produced personal computer with a graphical user interface.

While Kay's group was busy building the computer system of the future in its research lab, dozens of hobbyists gathered near San Francisco to found the Homebrew Computer Club, the first personal computer users group. They met to share ideas, programs, hardware, and applications for personal computing. The first mass-produced personal computer, the Altair, appeared in 1975. The Altair contained Intel's 8080 processor, the first *micro-computer* chip. But from the outside, the Altair looked and behaved more like a miniature version of the early computers than the Alto. Programs and their input had to be entered by flipping switches, and output was displayed by a set of lights. However, the Altair was small enough for personal computing enthusiasts to carry home, and I/O devices eventually were invented to support the processing of text and sound.

The Osborne and the Kaypro were among the first mass-produced interactive personal computers. They boasted tiny display screens and keyboards, with floppy disk drives for loading system software, applications software, and users' data files. Early personal computing applications were word processors, spreadsheets, and games such as Pacman and SpaceWar. These computers also ran CP/M (Control Program for Microcomputers), the first PC-based operating system.

In the early 1980s, a college dropout named Bill Gates and his partner Paul Allen built their own operating system software, which they called MS-DOS (Microsoft Disk Operating System). They then arranged a deal with the giant computer manufacturer IBM to supply MS-DOS for the new line of PCs that the company intended to mass-produce. This deal proved to be an advantageous one for Gates's company, Microsoft. Not only did Microsoft receive a fee for each computer sold, but it was able to get a head start on supplying applications software that would run on its operating system. Brisk sales of the IBM PC and its "clones" to individuals and institutions quickly made MS-DOS the world's most widely used operating system. Within a few years, Gates and Allen had become billionaires, and within a decade, Gates had become the world's richest man, a position he held for 13 straight years.

Also in the 1970s, the U.S. Government began to support the development of a network that would connect computers at military installations and research universities. The first such network, called ARPANET (Advanced Research Projects Agency Network), connected four computers at SRI, UCLA (University of California at Los Angeles), UC Santa Barbara, and the University of Utah. Bob Metcalfe, a researcher associated with Kay's group at Xerox, developed a software protocol called Ethernet for operating a network of computers. Ethernet allowed computers to communicate in a local area network (LAN) within an organization and with computers in other organizations via a wide area network (WAN). By the mid 1980s, the ARPANET had grown into what is now called the Internet, connecting computers owned by large institutions, small organizations, and individuals all over the world.

Communication and Media Computing (1990–2000)

In the 1990s, computer hardware costs continued to plummet, and processing speed and memory capacity skyrocketed. *Optical storage media* such as compact discs (CDs) and digital video discs (DVDs) were developed for mass storage. The computational processing of images, sound, and video became feasible and widespread. By the end of the decade, entire movies were being shot or constructed and played back using digital devices. The capacity to create lifelike three-dimensional animations of whole environments led to a new technology called *virtual reality*. New devices appeared, such as flatbed scanners and digital cameras, which could be used along with the more traditional microphone and speakers to support the input and output of almost any type of information.

Desktop and laptop computers not only performed useful work but gave their users new means of personal expression. This decade saw the rise of computers as communication devices, with email, instant messaging, bulletin boards, chat rooms, and the amazing World Wide Web.

Perhaps the most interesting story from this period concerns Tim Berners-Lee, the creator of the World Wide Web. In the late 1980s, Berners-Lee, a theoretical physicist doing research at the CERN Institute in Geneva, Switzerland, began to develop some ideas for using computers to share information. Computer engineers had been linking computers to networks for several years, and it was already common in research communities to exchange files and send and receive email around the world. However, the vast differences in hardware, operating systems, file formats, and applications still made it difficult for users who were not adept at programming to access and share this information. Berners-Lee was interested in creating a common medium for sharing information that would be easy to use, not only for scientists but for any other person capable of manipulating a keyboard and mouse and viewing the information on a monitor.

Berners-Lee was familiar with Vannevar Bush's vision of a web-like consultation system, Engelbart's work on NLS Augment, and the first widely available hypertext systems. One of these systems, Apple Computer's Hypercard, broadened the scope of hypertext to *hypermedia*. Hypercard allowed authors to organize not just text but images, sound, video, and executable applications into webs of linked information. However, a Hypercard database sat only on standalone computers; the links could not carry Hypercard data from one computer to another. Furthermore, the supporting software ran only on Apple's computers.

Berners-Lee realized that networks could extend the reach of a hypermedia system to any computers connected to the Internet, making their information available worldwide. To preserve its independence from particular operating systems, the new medium would need to have universal standards for distributing and presenting the information.

To ensure this neutrality and independence, no private corporation or individual government could own the medium and dictate the standards.

Berners-Lee built the software for this new medium, now called the World Wide Web, in 1992. The software used many of the existing mechanisms for transmitting information over the Internet. People contribute information to the web by publishing files on computers known as *web servers*. The web server software on these computers is responsible for answering requests for viewing the information stored on the web server. To view information on the web, people use software called a *web browser*. In response to a user's commands, a web browser sends a request for information across the Internet to the appropriate web server. The server responds by sending the information back to the browser's computer, called a *web client*, where it is displayed or rendered in the browser.

Although Berners-Lee wrote the first web server and web browser software, he made two other, even more important, contributions. First, he designed a set of rules, called HTTP (Hypertext Transfer Protocol), which allows any server and browser to talk to each other. Second, he designed a language, HTML (Hypertext Markup Language), which allows browsers to structure the information to be displayed on web pages. He then made all these resources available to anyone for free.

Berners-Lee's invention and gift of this universal information medium was a truly remarkable achievement. Today there are millions of web servers in operation around the world. Anyone with the appropriate training and resources—companies, government, nonprofit organizations, and private individuals—can start up a new web server or obtain space on one. Web browser software now runs not only on desktop and laptop computers, but on handheld devices such as cell phones.

Wireless Computing and Smart Devices (2000–Present)

The twenty-first century has seen the rise of wireless technology and the further miniaturization of computing devices. Today's smartphones allow you to carry enormous computing power around in your pocket and allow you to communicate with other computing resources anywhere in the world, via wireless or cellular technology. Tiny computing devices are embedded in cars and in almost every household appliance, from the washer/dryer and home theater system to the exercise bike. Your data (photos, music, videos, and other information) can now be stored in secure servers (the "cloud"), rather than on your devices.

Accompanying this new generation of devices and ways of connecting them is a wide array of new software technologies and applications. Only three very significant innovations are mentioned here.

In the late 1990s, Steve Jobs rejoined Apple Computer after an extended time away. He realized that the smaller handheld devices and wireless technology would provide a new way of delivering all kinds of "content"—music, video, books, and applications—to people.

To realize his vision, Jobs pursued the design and development of a handheld device with a clean, simple, and "cool" user interface to access this content. The first installment of such a device was the iPod, a music player capable of holding your entire music library as well as photos. Although the interface first used mechanical buttons and click wheels, it was soon followed by the iTouch, which employed a touch screen and could play video. The touch screen interface also allowed Apple and its programmers to provide *apps*, or special-purpose applications (such as games), that ran on these devices. When wireless connectivity became available, these apps could provide email, a web browser, weather channels, and thousands of other services. The iPhone and iPad, true multimedia devices with microphones, cameras, and motion sensors, followed along these lines a few years later.

Jobs also developed a new business model for distributing this content. Owners of these devices would connect to an e-store, such as the iTunes Store, the iBooks Store, and the App Store, to download free content or content for purchase. Authors, musicians, and app developers could upload their products to these stores in a similar manner. Thus, in a few short years, Jobs changed the way people consume, produce, and think about media content.

Also in the late 1990s, two Stanford University computer science graduate students, Larry Page and Sergey Brin, developed a powerful algorithm for searching the web. This algorithm served as the basis for a company they founded named Google. "To Google" is now a verb, synonymous with "to search on the web." Although people continue to browse or "surf" the web, much of what they do on the web is now based on search. In fact, most online research and many new industries would be inconceivable without search.

Finally, just after the turn of the millennium, a Harvard University undergraduate student named Mark Zuckerberg developed a prototype of the first social network program, which he called Facebook. The company he founded with the same name has changed the way that people connect to each other and present themselves online.

This concludes the book's not-so-brief overview of the history of computing. If you want to learn more about this history, run a web search or consult your local library. Now it's time for that introduction to programming in Python.

I Appreciate Your Feedback

I have tried to produce a high-quality text, but should you encounter errors, please report them to lambertk@wlu.edu. Any errata and other information about this book will be posted on the website http://home.wlu.edu/~lambertk/python/.

CHAPTER 1

GETTING STARTED WITH PYTHON

In this chapter, you explore some of Python's basic code elements. These code elements include operations on Python's basic types of data, such as numbers, strings, lists, and dictionaries. These data and operations form the building blocks of programs you will develop later in this book. The code presented in this chapter consists of simple fragments. As you read along, you are encouraged to run these code fragments in Python's interactive shell. Just remember that the best way to learn is to try things out yourself!

TAKING CARE OF PRELIMINARIES

In this section, you learn how to download Python and its documentation from its website, launch Python's IDLE shell, and evaluate Python expressions and statements within the shell.

Downloading and Installing Python

Some computer systems, such as Mac OS and Linux, come with Python already installed. Others, such as Windows, do not. In either case, you should visit Python's website at www.python.org/download/ to download the most current version of Python for your particular system. As of this writing, the most current version of Python is 3.3.4, but that number may be larger by the time you read these words.

While you are at Python's website, it's a good idea to download the documentation for your new version of Python, at www.python.org/doc/. You might also bookmark the link to the documentation for quick browsing online.

After downloading Python for your system, you install it by double-clicking on the installation file if you're a Mac or Windows user. Linux users have to unzip a source code package, compile it with GCC, and place it in the appropriate directory on their systems.

Launching and Working in the IDLE Shell

For the first three chapters of this book, you experiment with Python code in Python's IDLE shell. The shell displays a window in which you can enter program codes and obtain responses. The term IDLE stands for Integrated DeveLopment Environment. (It's also the last name of a Monty Python character, Eric Idle.) To launch IDLE in these three chapters, you run the command

```
idle3
```

in a terminal window. Before you do this, you must open or launch a terminal window, as follows:

- **Mac users**—Launch Terminal from the `Utilities` folder.
- **Windows users**—Launch a DOS window by entering the word `command` in the Start menu's entry box.
- **Linux users**—Right-click on the desktop and select Open Terminal.

Alternatively, Mac OS and Windows users can launch IDLE by double-clicking on the IDLE icon in the folder where your Python system is located. This folder is in the `Applications` folder in Mac OS and in the All Programs option of the Windows Start menu. You can create the appropriate shortcuts to these options for quick and easy access.

When you launch IDLE in a terminal window, you should see windows like the ones shown in Figure 1.1 (Mac OS version). Hereafter, the IDLE shell is simply called the *shell*.

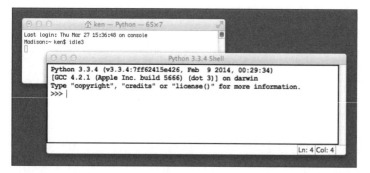

Figure 1.1
A new shell window.
© 2014 Python Software Foundation.

If the version number displayed in the shell is not 3.3.4 or higher, you need to close the shell window and download and install the current version of Python, as described earlier.

The shell provides a "sandbox" where you can try out simple Python code fragments. To run a code fragment, you type it after the >>> symbol and press the Return or Enter key. The shell then responds by displaying a result and giving you another >>> prompt. Figure 1.2 shows the shell and its results after the user has entered several Python code fragments.

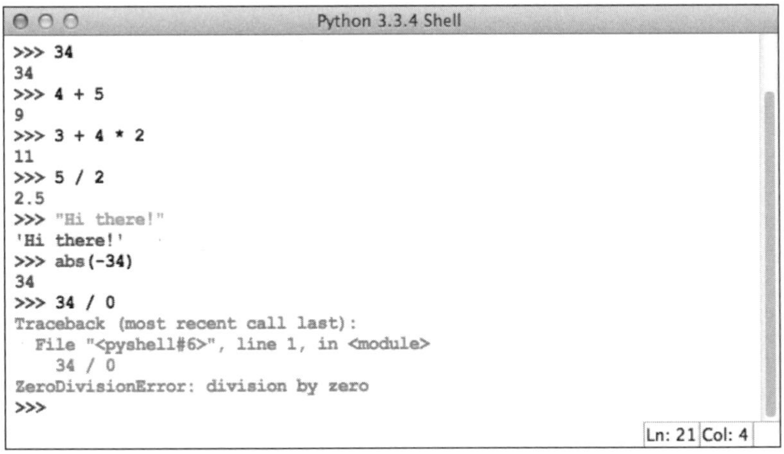

```
Python 3.3.4 Shell
>>> 34
34
>>> 4 + 5
9
>>> 3 + 4 * 2
11
>>> 5 / 2
2.5
>>> "Hi there!"
'Hi there!'
>>> abs(-34)
34
>>> 34 / 0
Traceback (most recent call last):
  File "<pyshell#6>", line 1, in <module>
    34 / 0
ZeroDivisionError: division by zero
>>>
                                         Ln: 21 Col: 4
```

Figure 1.2
The shell after entering several code fragments.
© 2014 Python Software Foundation.

Some of the text is color-coded (blue, green, and red) in your shell window, although these colors do not appear in this monochrome book. The colors indicate the roles of various code elements, to be described shortly.

To repeat the run of an earlier line of code, just place the cursor at the end of that line and press Return or Enter twice.

When you are ready to quit a session with the shell, you just select the shell window's close box or close the associated terminal window. However, keep a shell handy when reading this book, so you can try out each new idea as you encounter it.

Obtaining Python Help

There are two good ways to get help when writing Python code:

1. Browse the Python documentation.
2. Run Python's help function in the shell.

Python's `help` function is especially useful for getting quick help on basic code elements, such as functions. For example, the use of Python's `abs` function in Figure 1.2 might seem obvious to you, but if you're not sure, you can learn more by entering `help(abs)`, as shown in Figure 1.3.

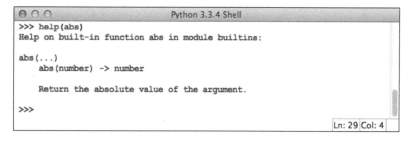

Figure 1.3
Getting help in the shell.
© 2014 Python Software Foundation.

WORKING WITH NUMBERS

Almost all computer programs use numbers in some way or another. In this section, you explore arithmetic with two basic types of numbers in Python: integers and floating-point numbers. Along the way, the important concepts of variables, assignment, functions, and modules are introduced.

Using Arithmetic

As you know from mathematics, *integers* are the infinite sequence of whole numbers {..., –2, –1, 0, 1, 2, ...}. Although this sequence is infinite in mathematics, in a computer program the sequence is finite and thus has a largest positive integer and a largest negative integer. In Python, the sequence of integers is quite large; the upper and lower bounds of the sequence depend on the amount of computer memory available.

Real numbers are numbers with a decimal point, such as 3.14 and 7.50. The digits to the right of the decimal point, called the *fractional part*, represent the *precision* of a real number. In mathematics, real numbers have infinite precision. The set of real numbers is also infinite. However, in a computer program, real numbers have an upper bound, a lower bound, and a finite precision (typically 16 digits). In Python and most other programming languages, real numbers are called *floating-point numbers*.

As you saw in the previous section, when you enter a number in the Python shell, Python simply displays that number; when you enter an arithmetic expression, Python evaluates and displays the value of that expression. Thus, the shell behaves like a pocket calculator (without the buttons). Python's basic arithmetic operations are listed in Table 1.1. In this table, the symbols A and B can be either numbers or expressions containing numbers and operators.

Table 1.1   Basic Arithmetic Operations

Operation	What It Does	Example	Value
A + B	Returns the sum of A and B	5 + 2	7
A - B	Returns the result of subtracting B from A	5 - 2	3
A * B	Returns the product of A and B	5 * 2	10
A / B	Returns the exact result of dividing A by B	5 / 2	2.5
A // B	Returns the integer quotient from dividing A by B	5 // 2	2
A % B	Returns the integer remainder from dividing A by B	5 % 2	1
A ** B	Returns A^B	5 ** 2	25
- A	Returns the arithmetic negation of A	- (5 * 2)	−10

Note the following points about the arithmetic operations:

1. The / operator produces the exact result of division, as a floating-point number.
2. The // operator produces an integer quotient.
3. When two integers are used with the other operators, the result is an integer.
4. When at least one floating-point number is used with the other operators, the result is a floating-point number. Thus, 5 * 2 is 10, whereas 5 * 2.3 is 11.5.

As in mathematics, the arithmetic operators are governed by *precedence rules*. If operators of the same precedence appear in consecutive positions, they are evaluated in left-to-right order. For example, the expression 3 + 4 - 2 + 5 is evaluated from left to right, producing 10.

When the operators do not have the same precedence, ** is evaluated first, then multiplication (*, /, //, or %), and finally addition (+ or -). For example, the expression 4 + 3 * 2 ** 3 first evaluates 2 ** 3, then 3 * 8, and finally 4 + 24, to produce 32.

You can use parentheses to override these rules. For example, (3 + 4) * 2 begins evaluation with the addition, whereas 3 + 4 * 2 begins evaluation with the multiplication. What are the results of evaluating these two expressions? Open a shell and check!

Negative numbers are represented with a minus sign. This sign is also used to negate more complex expressions, as in - (3 * 5). The precedence of the minus sign when used in this way is higher than that of any other arithmetic operator.

Table 1.2 shows the precedence of the arithmetic operators, where the operators of higher precedence are evaluated first.

Table 1.2   The Precedence of Arithmetic Operators

Operator	Precedence
- (unary negation)	4
**	3
*, /, //, %	2
+, - (binary subtraction)	1

The exponentiation operator ** is also *right associative*. This means that consecutive ** operators are evaluated from right to left. Thus, the expression 2 ** 3 ** 2 produces 512, whereas (2 ** 3) ** 2 produces 64.

Finally, a note on style: although Python ignores spaces within arithmetic expressions, the use of spaces around each operator can make your code easy for you and other people to read. For example, compare

```
34+67*2**6-3
```

to

```
34 + 67 * 2 ** 6 - 3
```

Working with Variables and Assignment

Suppose you are working on a program that computes and uses the volume of a sphere. You are given the sphere's radius of 4.2 inches. You first compute its volume using the formula $4/3\pi r^3$, with 3.1416 as your estimate of π. Here is the Python expression you might write for that:

```
4 / 3 * 3.1416 * 4.2 ** 3
```

If the value of this expression is used just once in your program, you compute it just once and use it there. However, if it is used in several places in your program, you must write the same expression several times. That's a waste of your time in writing code and a waste of the computer's time in evaluating it. Is there a way to write the expression, compute its value just once, and then simply use this value many times thereafter?

Yes, there is, and that's one reason why programs use *variables*. A variable in Python is a name that stands for a value. A Python variable is given a value by using the assignment operator =, according to the following form:

variable = expression

where *variable* is any Python name (with a few exceptions to be discussed later) and *expression* is any Python expression (including the arithmetic expressions under discussion here). Thus, in our example, the variable volume could be given the volume of the sphere via the assignment

volume = 4 / 3 * 3.1416 * 4.2 ** 3

and then used many times in other code later on. Note that because the precedence of assignment is lower that that of the other operators, the expression to the right of the = operator is evaluated first, before the variable to the left receives the value.

Now, suppose you had to compute the volumes of several different spheres. You could type out the expressions 4 / 3 and 3.1416 every time you write the code to compute a new volume. But you could instead use other variables, such as FOUR_THIRDS and PI, to make these values easy to remember each time you repeat the formula. Figure 1.4 shows a session in the shell where these values are established and the volumes of two spheres, with radii 4.2 and 5.4, are computed.

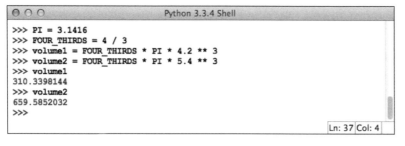

```
Python 3.3.4 Shell
>>> PI = 3.1416
>>> FOUR_THIRDS = 4 / 3
>>> volume1 = FOUR_THIRDS * PI * 4.2 ** 3
>>> volume2 = FOUR_THIRDS * PI * 5.4 ** 3
>>> volume1
310.3398144
>>> volume2
659.5852032
>>>
                                        Ln: 37 Col: 4
```

Figure 1.4
Using variables in code fragments.
© 2014 Python Software Foundation.

Python variables are spelled using letters, digits, and the underscore ('_'). The following rules apply to their use:

■ A variable must begin with a letter or an underscore ('_') and contain at least one letter.

■ Variables are case sensitive. Thus, the variable `volume` is different from the variable `Volume`, although they may refer to the same value.

■ Python programmers typically spell variables in lowercase letters but use capital letters or underscores to emphasize embedded words, as in `firstVolume` or `first_volume`.

■ When the value of a variable will not change after its initial assignment, it's considered a constant. `PI` is an example of a constant. Python programmers typically spell constants using all caps to indicate this.

■ Before you can use a variable, you must assign it a value. An attempt to use a variable that has not been initialized in this way generates an error message, as shown in Figure 1.5.

```
○ ○ ○                    Python 3.3.4 Shell
>>> volume1
310.3398144
>>> volume2
659.5852032
>>> volume3
Traceback (most recent call last):
  File "<pyshell#14>", line 1, in <module>
    volume3
NameError: name 'volume3' is not defined
>>>
                                              Ln: 42 Col: 4
```

Figure 1.5
Attempting to use a variable that has not been assigned a value.
© 2014 Python Software Foundation.

To summarize, there are three reasons to use variables in Python code:

1. They make code easy to read and understand.

2. They help to eliminate unnecessary computations.

3. They make code easy to modify and maintain (to be discussed later).

Using Functions

As you have seen, the arithmetic and assignment operations consist of an operator and one or more operands. Python also provides many other basic operations, which are packaged as *functions*. A function is like an operator but is referred to by a name rather than an operator symbol. When a function is evaluated or called, its operands are supplied to it in the form of *arguments*. For example, the Python function `abs` expects a number as its single argument and computes and returns that number's absolute value. Thus, the function call `abs(-34)` returns 34.

When a Python function is called, Python first evaluates its arguments. The resulting values are then passed to the function, which uses them to compute and return its value. Although the written form of a function call is slightly different, the process is no different from evaluating an expression with operands and operators. The form of a function call is as follows:

```
functionName(argumentExpression-1, argumentExpression-2, ...)
```

Function calls are expressions, and their arguments are expressions. For example, the arithmetic expression

```
abs(length - width) + 2
```

produces a result, as long as the variables `length` and `width` refer to numbers.

Some Python functions allow for optional arguments as well as required arguments. For example, the Python function `round` expects one required argument: the number to be rounded. If that number is a floating-point number, the integer value nearest to it is returned. However, `round` can also be called with a second argument: an integer indicating the number of places of precision to use in the result. Thus, `round(3.1416)` returns 3, whereas `round(3.1416, 3)` returns 3.142.

Generally, the number of arguments used with a function must match the number of its required arguments, unless it allows optional arguments. For functions provided by Python, the types of the arguments (such as numbers) used must also match the types of the arguments expected at each position in the sequence of arguments.

Using the math Module

Python's functions either are already available to call in the shell or must be imported from *modules* before use. A Python module is just a library of functions and other resources. There are many such modules, as you can see by browsing the `modules` index in the Python documentation. One of these is the `math` module, which contains useful functions for operations on numbers.

There are several ways to import a function from a module to make it available for use. The most common way is to use the form

```
import moduleName
```

where *moduleName* is the name of the module. When you have done this, you can call any function in the module by using the form

```
moduleName.functionName(sequenceOfArguments)
```

For example, suppose you want to compute the square root of 2. The following shell session shows how to do this:

```
>>> import math
>>> math.sqrt(2)
1.4142135623730951
```

Alternatively, if you prefer not to use the module name as a prefix in a function call, you can explicitly import the desired function, as follows:

```
>>> from math import sqrt
>>> sqrt(2)
1.4142135623730951
```

To view all the functions available in the `math` module, you run `dir(math)` after importing `math`, as follows:

```
>>> import math
>>> dir(math)
['__doc__', '__file__', '__loader__', '__name__', '__package__', 'acos', 'acosh', 'asin',
'asinh', 'atan', 'atan2', 'atanh', 'ceil', 'copysign', 'cos', 'cosh', 'degrees', 'e',
'erf', 'erfc', 'exp', 'expm1', 'fabs', 'factorial', 'floor', 'fmod', 'frexp', 'fsum',
'gamma', 'hypot', 'isfinite', 'isinf', 'isnan', 'ldexp', 'lgamma', 'log', 'log10',
'log1p', 'log2', 'modf', 'pi', 'pow', 'radians', 'sin', 'sinh', 'sqrt', 'tan', 'tanh',
'trunc']
```

If you have studied trigonometry, you should be able to spot the trigonometric functions, such as `cos` and `sin`, in this list. Note also that the variable `pi`, which is Python's name for the constant PI, is present. The value of this variable is Python's most precise estimate of π.

Now you can use this value to compute a more precise volume of a sphere than you did earlier, using the following statement:

```
volume = FOUR_THIRDS * math.pi * radius ** 3
```

Another way to access the items in a module is to import all of them explicitly. To do this with the `math` module, you run

```
from math import *
```

To access help on any module function, run the `help` function on the function's name. If you've imported just the module, you use the form

```
help(moduleName.functionName)
```

Otherwise, you use the form

```
help(functionname)
```

To get help on an entire module after importing it, run `help` on the module's name.

You might be thinking, "Hey, why doesn't the `math` module include a function to compute the volume of a sphere? Then I could just give that function the radius and let it do all the work." That would be a nice function to have, but the folks at python.org could not provide a function for every occasion. Later in this book, you learn how to create your own functions and modules to add to Python's built-in capabilities.

Detecting Errors

Figure 1.6 shows a shell session with several errors in Python code.

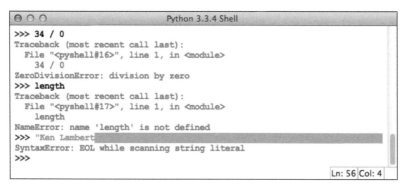

Figure 1.6
Examples of errors in Python code.
© 2014 Python Software Foundation.

There are three types of errors that can occur in your code:

- **Syntax errors**—These errors occur when your code is not well formed, according to the syntax or grammar rules of Python. For example, the expression `abs(-34)` is syntactically correct, but the expression `abs(-34))` is not. (It contains an extra right paren.)

- **Semantic errors**—These errors occur when a syntactically correct expression is evaluated, but Python cannot carry out the evaluation. For example, Python cannot divide a number by zero, cannot compute the square root of a negative number, and cannot use a variable that has not yet been given a value, even though you can enter each such expression in the shell without a syntax error.

- **Logic errors**—Also called *design errors*, these errors occur when Python successfully evaluates an expression, but the expression returns an incorrect result. For example, the expression `math.pi * 34 ** 2` does return a value, but if you expect this value to be the volume of a sphere of radius 34, your code contains a logic or design error.

Python detects syntax and semantic errors automatically and displays error messages. However, you must detect logic or design errors yourself by testing and inspecting the results of your code. In advanced software development settings, programmers can use software tools to automate some of this testing as well.

In general, you should regard error messages with a friendly eye and learn to understand what they mean. As you become a competent programmer, you will have few syntax and semantic errors in your code, so you can turn your attention to eliminating any logic errors.

WORKING WITH STRINGS

Text processing is almost as prevalent in computing as numerical processing. Instant messaging, texting, and word processing would be impossible without it. In this section, you explore working with strings, which form the basis of text processing.

String Literals

A *string* is a sequence of *characters*. The set of characters includes all the letters, digits, and punctuation marks that you see on a keyboard, as well as command or control characters and many others that don't appear there (such as the characters used in Arabic, Chinese, Greek, Japanese, Russian, and most other languages). In Python, *string literals* are represented as sequences of characters enclosed in quotes, as shown in the shell session in Figure 1.7.

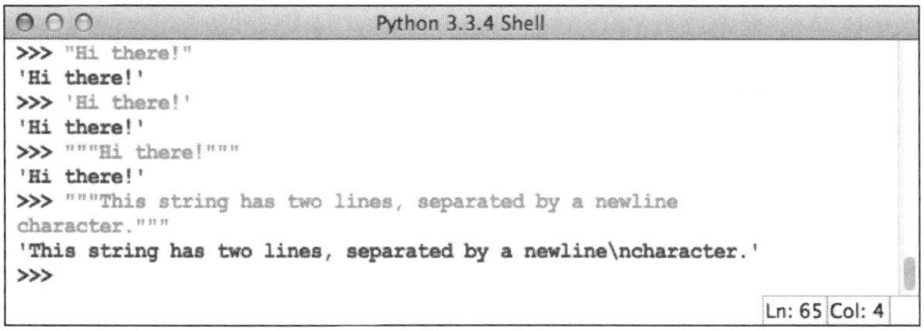

Figure 1.7
Examples of strings in Python.
© 2014 Python Software Foundation.

Note that you can use pairs of single quotes, pairs of double quotes, or pairs of triple-single or triple-double quotes. Strings enclosed in single quotes or double quotes cannot extend to the next line of code. Strings enclosed in triple quotes can extend to multiple lines of code, but the line breaks are included as characters within these strings.

Note also that, like numbers, strings evaluate to themselves, but the results are displayed in single quotes.

If you want to embed quotes within a string, you can place the escape character \ immediately before the embedded quote. The escape character is also used to embed special characters, such as the Tab and Return characters, within a string. Table 1.3 lists some escaped characters and their meanings.

Table 1.3 Some Escaped Characters

Character	Meaning
\n	Newline (Return or Enter)
\t	Horizontal Tab
\\	\
\'	'
\"	"

Strangely enough, the empty string, represented as "", is still a string, even though it contains no characters.

The len, str, int, and float Functions

A string's length is the number of characters it contains. The len function allows you to look up the length of its string argument, as shown in the next shell session:

```
>>> len("")
0
>>> len("Here are four words.")
20
```

Note that the empty string contains no characters, whereas the space counts as a character.

The str function converts its argument to a string representation. In the case of numbers, str has the effect of wrapping the number in a set of quote marks. The str function is often used to build text from other types of data values, such as numbers.

The int and float functions are used to build numbers from strings. Note that a string of digits does not look very different from a number that contains the same sequence of digits, but they are very different species of data from Python's point of view. The following shell session illustrates this difference and shows some uses of the int and float functions:

```
>>> 34 + 22
56
>>> "34" + "22"
'3422'
>>> "34" + 22
Traceback (most recent call last):
  File "<pyshell#10>", line 1, in <module>
    "34" + 22
TypeError: Can't convert 'int' object to str implicitly
>>> str(22)
'22'
>>> "34" + str(22)
'3422'
>>> int("34")
34
>>> int("34") + 22
56
>>> int(3.6)
3
>>> float(3)
3.0
```

Note that the int function does not round a floating-point number to the nearest integer but instead truncates or removes its fractional part.

Input and Output Functions

Computer programs typically take input data, process them, and output the results. In the program fragments you have seen thus far, the inputs are operands in expressions or arguments to functions, and the outputs are the values returned. When a program is not run from the Python shell but from a system terminal, separate input and output operations are needed to supply data to the program and display its results. For text-based terminal programs, Python provides two functions, named input and print, for this purpose. Although you will write very few such programs in this book, it's still a good idea to experiment with Python's input and print functions here, in "sandbox mode."

Output with the print Function

The print function expects zero or more arguments. It evaluates these arguments and converts their values to strings, builds a new string from them with single spaces between them, and displays this string as a single line of text. A line break is automatically displayed as well. The next shell session shows some examples of the use of the print function:

```
>>> print()

>>> print("Hello there!")
Hello there!
>>> print("Text followed by a blank line\n")
Text followed by a blank line

>>> print("Four uses the digit", 4)
Four uses the digit 4
```

Note that print has the effect of stripping off the quotes enclosing each string.

Input with the input Function

The input function expects an optional string as an argument. If the string is provided, the function displays it as a prompt for an input value and waits for the user to enter some keystrokes. When the user presses the Return or Enter key, the function builds and returns a string containing these keyboard characters. The next shell session shows some uses of the input function:

```
>>> input("Enter the radius: ")
Enter the radius: 7.55
'7.55'
>>> input("Press return to quit: ")
Press return to quit:
''
>>> name = input("Enter your name: ")
Enter your name: Ken Lambert
>>> name
'Ken Lambert'
```

Note that the minimal case of an input occurs when the user presses the Return or the Enter key, which produces the empty string.

When the user enters a string of digits for a number, the programmer must run the int or float function on this string before using the number in further computations. Here is an example, which inputs the length and width of a rectangle and outputs its area:

```
>>> width = int(input("Enter the width: "))
Enter the width: 34
>>> length = int(input("Enter the length: "))
Enter the length: 22
>>> print("The area is", width * length)
The area is 748
```

Indexing, Slicing, and Concatenation

Strings are *data structures*, which means they contain other data within them. Data structures provide operations for constructing a new datum from component parts and for accessing these parts after the datum has been constructed. The parts contained in a string are its characters, which themselves are other (single-character) strings. Thus, you should be able to build new strings out of existing strings and be able to access any of the characters or sequences of characters within a string.

Python builds a new string automatically when you enter a string literal in your code. You can also build new strings from existing strings by running the *concatenation operator +*. The next shell session shows some examples of string concatenation.

```
>>> "Ken" + "Lambert"
'KenLambert'
>>> "Ken" + " " + "Lambert"
'Ken Lambert'
```

```
>>> "" + "Not empty"
'Not empty'
>>> text = ""
>>> text = text + "Not empty"
>>> text
'Not empty'
```

The concatenation operator simply glues two strings together to form a new string. Note that the last assignment in this session shows that assignment is not the same thing as an equation in mathematics. A new string is built from the old one on the right side of the = operator, and then the variable text is reset to this new string. Python has a different operator, ==, that compares two values for equality, to be explored later.

The most basic string access operation is *indexing* or *subscripting*. This operation gives you the character at a given position in the string. Each character in a string has a definite position. These positions range from zero, the position of the first character, to the length of the string minus one, the position of the last character. The form of this operation is as follows:

aString[anIntegerIndexPosition]

The integer in square brackets following a string is also called a *subscript*, and the [] operator is called the *subscript operator*. Here is a shell session with some example subscript operations:

```
>>> name = "Ken Lambert"
>>> name
'Ken Lambert'
>>> name[0]
'K'
>>> name[len(name) - 1]
't'
>>> name[len(name)]
Traceback (most recent call last):
  File "<pyshell#13>", line 1, in <module>
    name[len(name)]
IndexError: string index out of range
```

The error on the last line results from giving an index position that lies beyond the sequence of positions in the string. Negative index values are allowed, counting from –1 (the last position) down to minus the length of the string (the first position).

The *slice* operation is similar to the index operation, but a range of positions is given, and a substring of characters is returned. The form of this operation is

aString[lowerBound:upperBound]

where *lowerBound* and *upperbound* are optional integer values. Here are some examples of slicing into a string:

```
>>> name = "Ken Lambert"
>>> name[:]
'Ken Lambert'
>>> name[0:]
'Ken Lambert'
>>> name[:len(name)]
'Ken Lambert'
>>> name[4:8]
'Lamb'
>>> name[4:]
'Lambert'
```

As you can see, when the lower bound is omitted, the substring begins with the first character in the string, and when the upper bound is omitted, the substring ends with the last character in the string. Otherwise, the substring begins with the character at the position of the lower bound and ends with the character at the position of the upper bound minus one.

Note that slicing, indexing, and concatenation do not modify the contents of existing strings because you cannot modify strings after you construct them.

String Methods

When you run `dir(str)` in the shell, you see all the string operations. They are called *methods*. Note that the method names at the beginning of this list contain underscores. These methods are associated with operators such as + and []. When Python sees an operator used with a string, it looks up the corresponding method and calls it with the appropriate arguments.

A method is like a function but has a slightly different calling protocol. When you run a method on a string, the string is written first, followed by a dot, followed by the method name and any of its arguments, as follows:

aString.methodName(argumentSequence)

Here are some example uses of string methods:

```
>>> "Ken Lambert".upper()
'KEN LAMBERT'
>>> "Ken Lambert".startswith('L')
```

```
False
>>> "44".isnumeric()
True
>>> "Ken Lambert".index('L')
4
>>> "Ken Lambert".split()
['Ken', 'Lambert']
```

You should be able to tell what these operations do just by examining the results. But if you're unsure of any of them, ask for help by entering help(str.*methodName*) in the shell.

WORKING WITH LISTS

People make and use lists of things for many different purposes, such as playlists of music or wish lists for shopping. In programming, you can create and process lists of numbers, strings, or any other data values. In this section, you explore the use of lists in Python.

List Literals and Operators

A *list* is a sequence of data values called *items*. Items can be any data values whatsoever. Like the characters in a string, the items in a list are ordered by position, counting from 0. In Python, a *list literal* is represented as a sequence of items separated by commas. The sequence of items is enclosed in square brackets, as shown in the next shell session.

```
>>> [34, 46, 22]
[34, 46, 22]
>>> emptyList = []
>>> len(emptyList)
0
>>> item1 = 34
>>> item2 = "Ken"
>>> listOfTwoItems = [item1, item2]
>>> listOfTwoItems
[34, 'Ken']
>>> listOfLists = [listOfTwoItems, emptyList]
>>> listOfLists
[[34, 'Ken'], []]
```

Note the following points about these lists:

- The empty list, [], contains no items and has a length of 0.
- Lists can contain other data structures, such as strings and lists.

- When an item in a list is a variable, the list actually contains the value of that variable. This technique of building a list is called *pattern matching*.

- Several variables can refer to the same list.

Lists generally support the same operators as strings. Thus, you can concatenate two lists with +, access an item at an index position with [], and get a slice of a list with [:]. In the case of the concatenation and slice operations, the results are always other lists.

However, unlike strings, lists can be modified after they are created. You can replace items at given positions, add them to an existing list, or remove them from an existing list. You replace an item at a given list position by placing a list subscript on the left side of an assignment statement, as shown in the following shell session:

```
>>> fruits = ["oranges", "bananas", "apples"]
>>> fruits
['oranges', 'bananas', 'apples']
>>> fruits[1] = "cherries"
>>> fruits
['oranges', 'cherries', 'apples']
```

Note that the integer index must range from minus the length of the list to the length of the list minus one. There are many other methods that modify lists, some of which are considered next.

List Methods

If you run dir(list) in the shell, you see all the list methods. Several of these are *index based*, meaning that they expect an integer index position as an argument. For example, the methods insert and pop are used to add and remove items at given positions, as shown here:

```
>>> fruits
['oranges', 'cherries', 'apples']
>>> fruits.insert(1, "peaches")
>>> fruits
['oranges', 'peaches', 'cherries', 'apples']
>>> fruits.pop(0)
'oranges'
>>> fruits
['peaches', 'cherries', 'apples']
>>> fruits.pop()
'apples'
>>> fruits
['peaches', 'cherries']
```

The insert method always inserts an item before the given index, after shifting some items to the right by one position. The pop method removes the item at the given index, before shifting some items to the left by one position. Note that when you omit the index, the pop method removes the last item in the list.

Other list methods are *content based*, meaning that they are given or targeted at an item rather than a position in the list. For example, the append method adds a given item to the end of a list, whereas the remove method removes the first instance of a given item from a list. The flowing shell session demonstrates these operations:

```
>>> fruits
['oranges', 'bananas', 'apples']
>>> fruits.append("grapes")
>>> fruits
['oranges', 'bananas', 'apples', 'grapes']
>>> fruits.remove("bananas")
>>> fruits
['oranges', 'apples', 'grapes']
```

Note that the item given to the remove method must already be in the list.

Although the items in a list are always ordered by position, they may not be in alphabetical order (if they are strings) or in ascending or descending order (if they are numbers). Rearranging list items into this kind of order is called *sorting*. Sorting is a complex process, but the list method sort makes that easy, as shown here:

```
>>> fruits
['oranges', 'peaches', 'cherries', 'apples']
>>> fruits.sort()
>>> fruits
['apples', 'cherries', 'oranges', 'peaches']
>>> grades
[77, 100, 85, 92]
>> grades.sort()
>>> grades
[77, 85, 92, 100]
>>> grades.reverse()
>>> grades
[100, 92, 85, 77]
```

Note that the methods sort and reverse are used in sequence to place list items in descending order.

Table 1.4 summarizes some commonly used list operations, where the variable L refers to a list.

Table 1.4 Some Commonly Used List Operations

List Operation	What It Does
len(L)	Returns the number of items currently in the list.
L[index]	Returns the item at the integer position index in the list. Note: do not use an index that is less than 0 or greater than or equal to the length of the list.
L[index] = item	Replaces the item at the integer position index in the list with item. Note: do not use an index that is less than 0 or greater than or equal to the length of the list.
L.append(item)	Adds item to the end of the list.
L.count(item)	Returns the number of instances of item in the list.
L.index(item)	Returns the position of the first instance of item in the list, or raises an exception if item is not present.
L.insert(index, item)	Inserts item at position index, shifting other items to the right by one position if necessary.
L.pop(index)	Removes the item at position index, shifting other items to the left by one position if necessary. If index is not provided, removes the item at the end of the list.
L.remove(item)	Removes the first instance of item in the list, or raises an exception if item is not present.

Lists from Other Sequences

Sometimes you'll want to build a new list from another sequence, such as a string or another list. The easiest way to do this is to supply that sequence as an argument to the list function, as follows:

```
>>> characters = list("Ken Lambert")
>>> characters
['K', 'e', 'n', ' ', 'L', 'a', 'm', 'b', 'e', 'r', 't']
>>> myCopy = list(characters)
>>> myCopy
['K', 'e', 'n', ' ', 'L', 'a', 'm', 'b', 'e', 'r', 't']
```

The first assignment creates a list of the characters in a string. The second assignment creates a copy of that list.

Another common way to build a list from a string is to use the string method split. This method returns a list of the words in the string, where the space character is the separator between the words. The original string can be reconstructed by running the string method join with the list of words as an argument. Here is an example:

```
>>> words = "Ken Lambert".split()
>>> words
['Ken', 'Lambert']
>>> " ".join(words)
'Ken Lambert'
```

Finally, to create a list from a range of numbers, you use Python's range function to create the range and pass this result to the list function.

Here are some examples:

```
>>> numbers = list(range(15))
>>> numbers
[0, 1, 2, 3, 4, 5, 6, 7, 8, 9, 10, 11, 12, 13, 14]
>>> oneThroughFifteen = list(range(1, 16))
>>> oneThroughFifteen
[1, 2, 3, 4, 5, 6, 7, 8, 9, 10, 11, 12, 13, 14, 15]
>>> fifteenThroughOne = list(range(15, 0, -1))
>>> fifteenThroughOne
[15, 14, 13, 12, 11, 10, 9, 8, 7, 6, 5, 4, 3, 2, 1]
```

When range gets a single integer argument, it returns a range of numbers from 0 to this integer minus one. When range gets two integer arguments, it returns a range from the first integer to the second integer minus one. When range gets three integer arguments, it returns a range from the first integer to the second integer minus one, but the value of the third integer is used to count the interval between the integers in the range. Thus, to count down rather than up, as in the example, the first integer must be greater than the second one, and the third integer must be negative.

Lists and the random Module

The set of integers is also a sequence, which allows you to treat other sets, such as the set of characters and the set of positions in a list or string, as sequences. You have seen that even when the items in a list or string are in a sequence, they may otherwise be in a random (unsorted) order. In many applications, you might want to arrange a set of items in a list in random order or perhaps select an item from a random position. (Think of shuffling a new deck of cards or picking a random ping pong ball from a bowl of such balls.) Python's `random` module includes some functions that allow you to perform these tasks with lists. The two most commonly used functions are `random.shuffle` and `random.choice`. Here are some uses of these two functions:

```
>>> import random
>>> numbers = list(range(1, 16))
>>> numbers
[1, 2, 3, 4, 5, 6, 7, 8, 9, 10, 11, 12, 13, 14, 15]
>>> random.shuffle(numbers)
>>> numbers
[6, 11, 1, 12, 3, 10, 13, 4, 5, 15, 2, 7, 9, 8, 14]
>>> random.choice(numbers)
13
>>> random.choice(numbers)
8
>>> coin = ["heads", "tails"]
>>> random.choice(coin)
'heads'
>>> random.choice(coin)
'heads'
>>> random.choice(coin)
'tails'
```

Tuples as Immutable Lists

You saw earlier that a string is *immutable*, meaning that its contents and structure cannot change after it is created. You also saw that lists are *mutable*, meaning that you can alter their contents and structure with replacements, insertions, and removals. Although lists are mutable, occasionally you want to create sequences of items that are list-like but also immutable. In Python, a data structure called a *tuple* fills this bill.

A tuple looks just like a list but uses parentheses rather than square brackets to enclose its items. Tuples are created by mentioning them as literals (with possibly embedded variables) or by running the `tuple` function on another sequence, such as a list, a string, or a range of numbers. The usual operators have the expected results, but a tuple with a sub-script cannot appear on the left side of an assignment. The next shell session shows some examples:

```
>>> pair = (1, 2)
>>> triple = (3, 4, 5)
>>> len(triple)
3
>>> triple[2]
5
>>> triple[1:]
(4, 5)
>>> pair + triple
(1, 2, 3, 4, 5)
>>> tuple(range(15))
(0, 1, 2, 3, 4, 5, 6, 7, 8, 9, 10, 11, 12, 13, 14)
>>> tuple("Ken Lambert".split())
('Ken', 'Lambert')
```

WORKING WITH DICTIONARIES

Lists and tuples are sequences. They are well suited for applications in which items must be ordered by position. Another type of data structure, called the *dictionary*, does not order its items by position. Instead, a dictionary associates each item with a unique value called a *key*. For example, when you hear the words *mother* and *father*, it's likely that images of your mother and father immediately come to mind. In a crude sense, your mind or memory is like a big dictionary, in which each item or idea is associated with a unique key that allows you to access it. In this section, you explore the use of Python dictionaries to model this type of memory storage.

Dictionary Literals

A dictionary is a set of key/value pairs. In a Python dictionary, the keys must be unique, but the values can be repeated. A key must be an immutable value, such as a number or a string. A value can be any Python data object or even a function or method.

A dictionary literal consists of curly braces {}, which enclose a sequence of key/value pairs. Commas separate the pairs. Within each pair, a colon appears between the key and the value. The next shell session shows some example dictionaries:

```
>>> {}
{}
>>> kenInfo = {"name":"Ken", "hair-color":"gray", "age":63}
```

```
>>> kenInfo
{'hair-color': 'gray', 'name': 'Ken', 'age': 63}
>>> list(kenInfo.keys())
['hair-color', 'name', 'age']
>>> list(kenInfo.values())
['gray', 'Ken', 63]
>>> list(kenInfo.items())
[('hair-color', 'gray'), ('name', 'Ken'), ('age', 63)]
>>> elvisInfo = dict([("name", "Elvis"), ("hair-color", "black"), ("age", 22)])
>>> elvisInfo
{'hair-color': 'black', 'name': 'Elvis', 'age': 22}
```

Dictionary Methods and Operators

Note the use of the keys, values, and items methods to pick out the dictionary's keys, values, and key/value pairs, respectively. Like other data structures, a dictionary is created when it's mentioned as a literal, or when you run the dict function with the appropriate argument—in this case, a list of tuples. The len function returns the number of keys in a dictionary, but the + operator is undefined.

There are two basic access operations. One operation just places a target key in a subscript operator, as in

```
>>> elvisInfo["name"]
'Elvis'
```

and the value associated with that key is returned. However, if the key is absent, Python displays an error message. To avoid that potential problem, you can run the get method on the dictionary, with the purported key and a default value to be returned if that key is not found, as follows:

```
>>> elvisInfo.get("weight", None)
None
```

The pop method, like get, expects two arguments: a key and a default value to return if the key is absent. If the key exists, Python removes the key and its associated value and returns the value; otherwise, the default value is returned.

When a subscript appears with a dictionary on the left side of an assignment, it is used as either a replacement or an insertion operation. Here is an example:

```
>>> ringoInfo = {}
>>> ringoInfo["name"] = "Ringo"
>>> ringoInfo["profession"] = "drummer"
```

```
>>> ringoInfo
{'profession': 'drummer', 'name': 'Ringo'}
>>> ringoInfo["profession"] = "retired"
>>> ringoInfo
{'profession': 'retired', 'name': 'Ringo'}
```

As you can see, the first two assignments access keys for the first time, so they serve as insertions. The third assignment performs a replacement of a value at a given key.

Table 1.5 summarizes some commonly used dictionary operations, where the variable D refers to a dictionary.

Table 1.5 Some Commonly Used Dictionary Operations

Dictionary Operation	What It Does
len(D)	Returns the number of keys currently in the dictionary.
D[key]	Returns the value at key in the dictionary. Note: do not use a key that is not in the dictionary.
D[key] = value	Replaces the value at key in the dictionary with value, if key is in the dictionary. Otherwise, inserts key and value into the dictionary.
D.get(key, defaultValue)	Returns the value at key, or defaultValue if key is not present.
D.pop(key, defaultValue)	Removes and returns the value at key, or defaultValue if key is not present.

This concludes your introduction to Python basics. After doing the exercises for this chapter, you will be ready to explore turtle graphics programming in Python.

SUMMARY

- The Python shell provides a playspace for entering Python code, running it, and viewing the results.

- Basic Python data types include integers, floating-point numbers, strings, lists, tuples, and dictionaries.

- Python arithmetic operators include addition (+ and -), multiplication (*, /, and %), and exponentiation (**).

- A Python function is an operation that can be called by name to produce a value. When a function is called, it can receive other data as arguments to use in its computations.

- A Python module, like the `math` module, is a library of functions and other resources that can be imported for use in your code. Examples of these resources are the function `math.sqrt` and the constant `math.pi`.

- The `int`, `float`, and `str` functions are used to convert data to integers, floating-point numbers, and strings, respectively.

- Python variables are names that refer to data values.

- The assignment operator `=` is used to set a variable to a value.

- A data structure is a datum that contains other data values. Operations exist to construct data structures and to access their component parts. Examples of data structures are strings, lists, tuples, and dictionaries.

- A string is a sequence of zero or more characters. Python strings appear enclosed in quote marks.

- The `+` operator glues together two strings to build a new string that contains them. This operation is called concatenation.

- The `[]` operator returns the character at the given integer index position in a string.

- The `[]` operator returns a substring of a string when a `":"` appears within the operator. This is known as a slice operation.

- A list is a sequence of zero or more data values. The items in Python lists appear enclosed in square brackets. Lists respond to the `+` and `[]` operators, as well as operations to insert and remove items. Unlike strings, lists are mutable.

- A tuple is a sequence of zero or more data values. The items in Python tuples appear enclosed in parentheses. Unlike lists, tuples are immutable.

- A dictionary is a set of key/value pairs. The items in Python dictionaries appear enclosed in curly braces. The data within a dictionary are not ordered by their positions, but by their keys.

- The named operations on strings, lists, tuples, and dictionaries are known as methods. A method call consists of a datum, followed by a dot, followed by the method's name and a parenthesized list of arguments.

EXERCISES

Launch the Python shell and complete the following exercises.

1. Enter expressions that compute the area of a circle, the volume of a sphere, and the surface area of a sphere. You should use the variable radius with the same value in each of these expressions, as well as the most precise value of π available in Python.

2. Enter an assignment statement that sets the variable name to your full name. Then enter an expression that uses this variable and the slice operator to return your last name.

CHAPTER 2

GETTING STARTED WITH TURTLE GRAPHICS

Python's basic code elements allow you to manipulate numbers, text, and data structures such as lists and dictionaries. However, modern computers also make extensive use of graphics and allow you to interact with graphical images directly by moving a mouse or pointing device. In this chapter, you learn some basic Python graphics operations, using a subsystem called turtle graphics.

LOOKING AT THE TURTLE AND ITS WORLD

Turtle graphics was developed with the Logo programming language in the late 1960s to teach programming to children. Turtle graphics allows you to simulate the movements of a turtle robot by moving an image around on a computer monitor. The turtle is equipped with a pen that can draw lines and shapes as it moves about.

The turtle has a position in a two-dimensional coordinate system. In geometry, a two-dimensional coordinate system consists of a horizontal x-axis and a vertical y-axis, as shown in Figure 2.1.

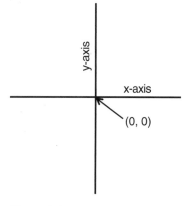

Figure 2.1
A two-dimensional coordinate system.

The origin or center point of this system, (0, 0), is located at the intersection of the axes. Any other position (x, y) is relative to the origin. The x values are positive to the right of the origin and negative to the left of it. The y values are positive above the origin and negative below it.

You can move the turtle forward or backward a given distance from its current position. The direction of this movement is determined by its current heading. You can turn its heading a given number of degrees to the left or to the right. You can also set the turtle pen's color and size, draw some basic shapes, fill those shapes with color, control the turtle's speed, and access the boundaries of the turtle's drawing area.

To experiment with turtle graphics in the Python shell, launch IDLE as you did in Chapter 1, "Getting Started with Python." Then run the following code fragments in the shell:

```
>>> from turtle import *
>>> showturtle()
```

You should see a second window pop up, like the one shown in Figure 2.2.

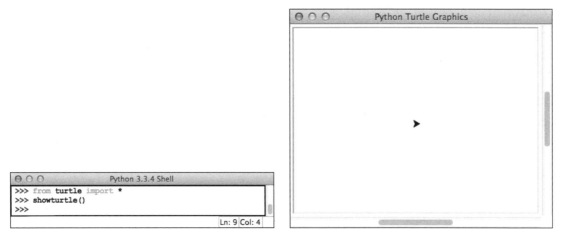

Figure 2.2
The turtle at home in its window.
© 2014 Python Software Foundation.

If the turtle graphics window is too large, you can resize it in the usual manner. Note that the turtle's image or shape is a caret symbol, and its initial heading is due east, or 0 degrees.

The import statement makes all the turtle graphics operations available to run as function calls. The showturtle function displays the turtle at its current position. The turtle's initial position is (0, 0) in the coordinate system. Note that this position, also called the *home position*, is at the center of the turtle graphics window.

The turtle has a number of attributes, whose initial values are listed in Table 2.1.

Table 2.1   Some of the Turtle's Initial Settings

Attribute	Initial Value
fillcolor	"black"
heading	0 degrees (due east)
pencolor	"black"
pensize	1 (pixel unit)
position	(0, 0)
shape	"classic" (the caret symbol)
speed	3 (0 is the fastest; 10 is the slowest)

You should arrange the shell and turtle graphics windows so that they are side by side on your computer monitor, as shown in Figure 2.2. You can then enter commands in the shell and view the results in the other window.

You might be wondering why you see a caret symbol rather than an image of a turtle. If you prefer to see a turtle, you can change the turtle's shape. To do that, return to the shell and enter the command shape("turtle"). The new shape is shown in Figure 2.3.

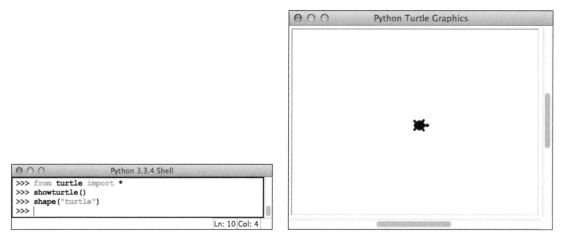

Figure 2.3
Changing the turtle's shape.
© 2014 Python Software Foundation.

When you have finished a session with turtle graphics, you can quit by closing the turtle graphics window and then the shell window.

As you work through the rest of this chapter, be sure that you can access the turtle graphics documentation at Python's website. The turtle module documentation is in the Global Modules Index of Python's documentation (http://docs.python.org/3/library/turtle.html#module-turtle). Appendix A, "Turtle Graphics Commands," also documents the commonly used turtle graphics operations.

USING BASIC MOVEMENT OPERATIONS

In this section, you pick up where you left off after showing the turtle in the previous section. You learn various ways of moving the turtle around to draw some geometric shapes.

Moving and Changing Direction

After you run the following commands in the shell, the results should appear as shown in Figure 2.4:

```
>>> left(45)
>>> forward(64)
>>> position()
(45.25,45.25)
>>> heading()
45.0
```

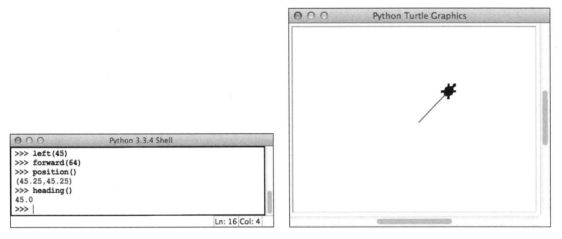

Figure 2.4
The turtle turns and moves to a new position.

Note that turning the turtle to the left rotates it counterclockwise by a given number of degrees. When you move it 64 units in the current direction, the turtle's pen draws a line segment that ends at position (45.25, 45.25). Most of the turtle graphics functions either tell the turtle to do things or return information about its current situation.

Now, you might be asking yourself, "Why is there no reference to the turtle in my Python code? Why didn't I have to pass a turtle datum as an argument to those functions, like I did with numbers and other data in Chapter 1?"

The nice thing about getting started with turtle graphics is that you just run the basic functions without worrying about things like this. Python takes care of directing these commands to a single "system" turtle underneath the hood. When you start to work with multiple turtles later in this book, you learn how to identify them so you can manipulate them separately.

If at any point you want to clear all the turtle's drawings and return the turtle to its initial position and heading, you just call the reset function.

When you start turtle graphics, the turtle's pen is initially down on the canvas, ready to draw lines and shapes. You can pick the pen up and put it down by calling the up and down functions, respectively. When the pen is up, you can move the turtle without drawing anything.

Drawing a Square

The basic turtle movement functions are listed in Table 2.2.

Table 2.2 Turtle Movement Functions

Function	What It Does
backward(distance)	Moves the turtle the given distance in the opposite of its current direction
forward(distance)	Moves the turtle the given distance in its current direction
goto(x, y)	Moves the turtle to position (x, y)
home()	Moves the turtle to position (0, 0) and sets its heading to 0 degrees
left(degrees)	Turns the turtle counterclockwise by the given degrees
right(degrees)	Turns the turtle clockwise by the given degrees
setheading(degrees)	Sets the turtle's heading to degrees

There are also several synonyms for these functions, which you can look up in the documentation. Note that the functions forward, backward, left, and right adjust the turtle's position or heading relative to its current position or heading. By contrast, the functions goto, home, and setheading reset the turtle's position or heading directly.

To explore some of these operations, you'll examine two ways to draw a square of length 70 with the turtle. Assume that the lower-left corner of this square is at the home position. The desired result is shown in Figure 2.5.

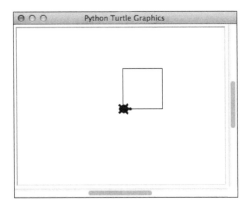

Figure 2.5
Drawing a square.
© 2014 Python Software Foundation.

The first method uses the reset, forward, and left functions. The reset function positions the turtle at the lower-left corner of the square, heading east. Now imagine that you are the turtle, standing on the drawing area and heading east. You would walk forward 70 units, turn left 90 degrees, walk forward again, and turn left again. You'd perform these two steps twice more until you were back at the home position. Here is the code that describes this process and carries it out in turtle graphics:

```
>>> reset()
>>> forward(70)
>>> left(90)
>>> forward(70)
>>> left(90)
>>> forward(70)
>>> left(90)
>>> forward(70)
>>> left(90)
```

Note that the last call of the left function is not necessary to complete the drawing, but it leaves the turtle's heading as it was at the beginning of the process.

The second method uses the goto function to draw line segments between each of the four corners of the square. To do this, you must first figure out the positions of the four corners. They are (0, 0), (70, 0), (70, 70), and (0, 70). These coordinates give the arguments to the four calls of goto required to draw the square, as follows:

```
>>> reset()
>>> goto(70, 0)
>>> goto(70, 70)
>>> goto(0, 70)
>>> goto(0, 0)
```

Note that `goto` does not change the turtle's heading.

Which method seems easier and more straightforward to you? The first method probably requires less mental effort; aside from knowing that each corner of a square encloses a 90-degree angle, you just have to know the number of sides and the length of a side. The second method forces you to calculate all the coordinates of the corners ahead of time. Moreover, if you want to change the length of the square the next time you draw it, you only have to change one value in the first method: the length of the square. At times, you will want to use `goto`, but this is not one of them.

Drawing an Equilateral Triangle

Now consider drawing an equilateral triangle. In this type of triangle, all the sides are the same length, and each vertex forms an interior angle of 60 degrees. If you assume that the length is 70 units, the leftmost vertex is at the origin, and the top vertex is above the x-axis, then the triangle is as shown in Figure 2.6.

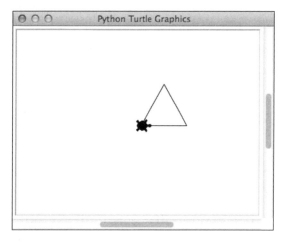

Figure 2.6
Drawing an equilateral triangle.
© 2014 Python Software Foundation.

How would you draw this triangle? Each vertex of the triangle encloses an angle of 60 degrees. So, following the preferred method for drawing a square, if you move the turtle forward 70 units and turn left 60 degrees three times, that should do it, right? Unfortunately, the result shown in Figure 2.7 doesn't quite cut it.

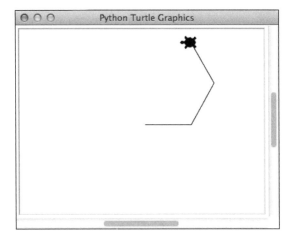

Figure 2.7
A failed attempt to draw an equilateral triangle.
© 2014 Python Software Foundation.

This is a good example of a logic or design error. You meant to create an interior angle of 60 degrees by turning left 60 degrees, but you got an interior angle of 120 degrees instead. To get the correct result, you need to turn further, exactly 120 degrees, each time. Recall that drawing a square requires four left turns of 90 degrees each, or 360 total degrees. The total number of degrees turned by the turtle in its circuit for an equilateral triangle is also 360 degrees (3 turns of 120 degrees each). You will use this fact about turtle geometry to draw some other geometric shapes in the exercises.

Undoing, Clearing, and Resetting

When you edit a file of text, the Edit menu typically offers an Undo Typing option. When you select this option, the editor deletes the word or phrase that you most recently entered. In a similar fashion, turtle graphics keeps track of all the commands that you enter and allows you to undo the most recent command by calling the undo function. Thus, instead of clearing the canvas, you can back up just a bit if you don't like the results by entering one or more undo commands.

If you don't like the results at all, or you just want to clear a drawing and start over, you can call clear or reset. Both functions erase all the drawings on the canvas. However, clear leaves all the turtle's current settings alone (position, heading, color, and pen size), whereas reset restores the turtle's initial settings.

SETTING AND EXAMINING THE TURTLE'S STATE

You have seen how the turtle has some initial settings when the turtle graphics window opens: a position, a heading, and a pen color. These and various other values are called the turtle's *state*. The turtle functions either change the turtle's state or allow you to examine it. In this section, you explore three other aspects of the turtle's state: its pen size, its shape, and its speed.

The Pen Size

The turtle's pen draws lines by painting tiny colored squares at various positions. These squares are called *pixels*. If your monitor has a high resolution, these pixels are quite tiny, so the lines drawn appear very thin. This is okay for fine work, but you might want to increase the pen's size to draw heavier lines otherwise. To do so, you call the pensize function with the new pen size as an integer argument. For example, the expression pensize(4) sets the pen's size to 4 pixels. To look up the current pen size, you call pensize().

The Shape

As you saw earlier, the turtle's shape is initially a caret symbol. You can change the turtle's shape to any of the built-in shapes provided by turtle graphics, or you can add a new shape of your own. Table 2.3 lists the names and icons of the standard turtle shapes. The function getshapes returns a list of the available shape names.

Table 2.3   The Built-in Turtle Shapes and Their Names

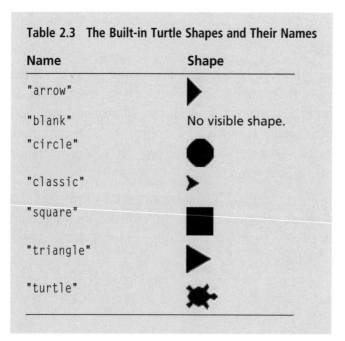

Name	Shape
"arrow"	▶
"blank"	No visible shape.
"circle"	●
"classic"	➤
"square"	■
"triangle"	▶
"turtle"	🐢

To change the turtle's shape, simply call the shape function with the desired shape name as a string argument. For example, the expression shape("turtle") changes the turtle's shape to a turtle. Calling shape with no argument returns the turtle's current shape name. If you do not want to see the turtle's shape, simply call hideturtle() or change its shape to "blank".

The function addshape adds a new shape to the set of shapes already in turtle graphics. You can use an image you have created for the new shape as long as its file is in GIF format. You then give addshape the name of this file as an argument. For example, if you want the turtle's shape to be the Trident, the logo of Washington and Lee University, you run the following code. The result is shown in Figure 2.8.

```
>>> addshape("trident.gif")
>>> getshapes()
['arrow', 'blank', 'circle', 'classic', 'square', 'triangle',
'trident.gif', 'turtle']
>>> shape("trident.gif")
```

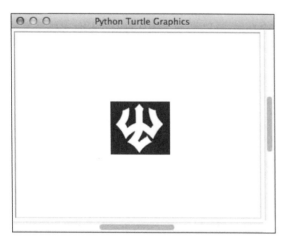

Figure 2.8
Changing the turtle's shape to the Trident.
© 2014 Python Software Foundation.

Python looks in the current working directory for the shape's file. If the file is somewhere else, you must provide its full pathname. If you want to find the pathname of the current working directory, run the following code:

```
>>> import os
>>> os.getcwd()
'/Users/ken/Documents'
```

Note that the string returned is the pathname of the Documents folder on my computer. If I put the file for the shape in that folder, Python can locate it with just the file's name.

You can also create your own shapes for the turtle with Python's shape and poly functions. Check the documentation for details.

The Speed

You can see the turtle move when it draws a line. If the turtle moves too slowly, you might get impatient with it, but if it moves too quickly, you might not be able to observe its movement. The function speed allows you to set the turtle's speed to your satisfaction. The argument to speed can be either an integer or a string. The integers range from 0 to 10, with 0 being the fastest speed. The other integers decrease the speed, from 10 down to 1. The turtle's initial speed is 3. Table 2.4 lists the available strings for speeds and the corresponding integers. As usual, calling the function with no argument returns the current speed.

Table 2.4 Turtle Speed Values as Strings and Integers

String	Integer
"fastest"	0
"fast"	10
"normal"	6
"slow"	3
"slowest"	1

Other Information About the Turtle's State

As you have seen, when you call the functions pensize, shape, and speed without arguments, these functions return the current values of these settings. You can obtain information about any aspect of the turtle's state by calling the appropriate function. For instance, try calling the functions position, heading, isdown, and isvisible. You will use this information in turtle graphics applications later in this book.

WORKING WITH COLORS

Color monitors support the display of bright and beautiful drawings and images. Although the turtle's initial color is black and the color of the canvas is white, you can reset these colors to any color that your system supports.

The Pen Color and the Background Color

The easiest way to change the pen's color is to call the `pencolor` function with a string argument. Example strings are the names of common colors, such as `"red"` or `"green"`. You can change the color of the canvas by calling the `bgcolor` function in a similar manner. Figure 2.9 shows a white square drawn on a black background after changing the initial pen and background colors.

Figure 2.9
Drawing with a white pen on a black background.
© 2014 Python Software Foundation.

Note that when you change the pen color, the turtle's shape also assumes that color.

Millions of other colors are available on modern computer systems. To use these, you need to learn how computers represent colors.

How Computers Represent Colors

All data used in computers are ultimately represented as numbers. Integers and floating-point numbers are obvious examples. The characters contained in strings translate to integer values that are stored and manipulated within the computer. Colors are no different. Each of the shades of the basic colors that you see, and all the mixtures thereof, must be translated by input devices such as scanners and cameras to numbers before you can store and process them. Before colors are displayed on a monitor, the computer must translate these numbers back to the colors that you see.

Among the various schemes for representing colors, the *RGB system* is a fairly common one. The letters stand for the color components of red, green, and blue, to which the human retina is sensitive. These components are mixed to form a unique color value. Naturally, the computer represents these values as integers. A color component can be any integer from 0 through 255. The value 255 represents the maximum intensity of a given color component, whereas the value 0 represents the total absence of that component. The RGB value (0, 0, 0) is black, and the RGB value (255, 255, 255) is white. Table 2.5 lists some example colors and their RGB values.

Table 2.5 Some Colors and Their RGB Values

Color	RGB Value
`"black"`	(0, 0, 0)
`"red"`	(255, 0, 0)
`"green"`	(0, 255, 0)
`"blue"`	(0, 0, 255)
`"yellow"`	(255, 255, 0)
`"gray"`	(127, 127, 127)
`"white"`	(255, 255, 255)

In Python, an RGB value is represented as the tuple (r, g, b). There are 256^3 or 16,777,216 distinct colors in this system—so many that the human eye cannot distinguish many of the adjacent values.

To set the pen color or background color to an RGB value, you first have to set the turtle's color mode to 255 by calling `colormode(255)`. You then can call `pencolor` or `bgcolor` with three integer arguments or with a single tuple of three integers. For example, `pencolor(127, 0, 0)` sets the pen color to maroon.

For more information on colors, consult PageTutor's ColorPicker site, at www.pagetutor.com/colorpicker/index.html.

Filled Shapes

Earlier you saw how to draw a square with the turtle. Suppose you want to draw not just the outline of a square, but a square filled with a given color. Turtle graphics allows you to do so by using the fillcolor, begin_fill, and end_fill functions.

You begin by setting the fill color of the shape. The fillcolor function does this using a color argument, as discussed in the previous section. The initial fill color is black. Note that when you set the fill color, this color also fills the shape of the turtle.

You then call the begin_fill function, followed by the commands that draw the square. Finally, you call the end_fill function, which tells turtle graphics to fill any fillable shapes drawn since the last call of begin_fill. The next session draws a filled square of length 70, with a black outline and a red interior. The result is shown in Figure 2.10 (color omitted, of course).

```
>>> reset()
>>> fillcolor("red")
>>> begin_fill()
>>> forward(70)
>>> left(90)
>>> forward(70)
>>> left(90)
>>> forward(70)
>>> left(90)
>>> forward(70)
>>> left(90)
>>> end_fill()
```

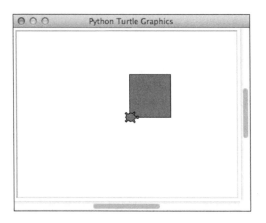

Figure 2.10
Drawing a filled shape.
© 2014 Python Software Foundation.

The `color` function combines actions of the `pencolor` and `fillcolor` functions. Its first argument is the pen color, and its second argument is the fill color. When called with no arguments, `color` returns a tuple containing these two colors. Thus, the expression `color("blue", "red")` would set the pen color to blue and the fill color to red.

Table 2.6 summarizes the functions related to colors in turtle graphics.

Table 2.6 Functions Related to Colors

Function	What It Does
bgcolor(color)	Sets the color of the canvas to color
color(pColor, fColor)	Sets the turtle's pen color to pColor and its fill color to fColor
fillcolor(color)	Sets the turtle's fill color to color
pencolor(color)	Sets the turtle's pen color to color
begin_fill()	Begins a sequence of commands to draw filled shapes
end_fill()	Ends a sequence of commands to draw filled shapes

DRAWING CIRCLES

Turtle graphics provides just one built-in function that draws a shape. This function, named `circle`, expects the circle's radius as an argument. Optional arguments include the `extent` (the portion of the circle to be drawn, in degrees) and the `steps` (the number of lines used to draw the circle's circumference). You supply the `extent` argument when you want to draw an arc. Filling an arc requires you to connect the turtle's starting and ending points.

To get a feel for how the circle function works, run the following code in the shell:

```
>>> from turtle import *
>>> home()
>>> circle(50)
```

Note that the turtle starts by facing east at the home position, draws the circle by repeatedly moving forward and turning left, and finally returns to its original position and heading.

Now consider how to draw a filled pie slice within this circle. The slice is a filled arc that occupies the lower-right quarter of the circle, as shown in Figure 2.11.

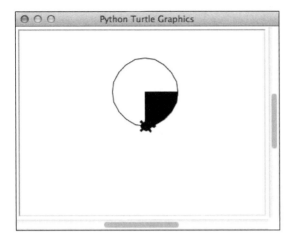

Figure 2.11
Drawing a circle containing a filled arc.
© 2014 Python Software Foundation.

You start by running `begin_fill` to begin drawing a filled shape. To draw the arc, the turtle starts at the home position and draws a circle with a radius of 50 and an extent of 90 degrees. The turtle then draws two line segments to close the arc, create the pie slice, and allow it to be filled. To do this, you move the turtle to position (0, 50), which is the center point of the circle, and then return it to the home position. Finally, you run `end_fill` to fill the new shape. Here is the code:

```
>>> begin_fill()
>>> circle(50, 90)
>>> goto(0, 50)
>>> home()
>>> end_fill()
```

The key to working with circles and arcs is to set the initial position and the heading of the turtle to get the results that you want. For example, suppose you want a half-moon shape whose center point is the origin, whose radius is 50, and whose flat side lies along the x-axis, as shown in Figure 2.12.

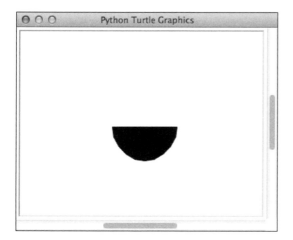

Figure 2.12
Drawing a half moon.
© 2014 Python Software Foundation.

The turtle starts drawing the circle from position (–50, 0), with the turtle's heading at 270 degrees. Moving to that position from the home position draws half of the flat side of the arc. Then the turtle turns right 90 degrees. To draw the arc, the turtle draws the circle with an extent of 180 degrees. After drawing the arc, the turtle draws the other half of its flat side by returning home. Here is the code:

```
>>> reset()
>>> begin_fill()
>>> goto(-50, 0)
>>> right(90)
>>> circle(50, 180)
>>> home()
>>> end_fill()
>>> hideturtle()
```

DRAWING TEXT

You draw text in the turtle's window by calling the write function. The required argument is a string. Optional arguments direct the turtle to move during the drawing, align the text to the left, center, or right of the turtle's initial position, and use a text font that you supply. The following code fragments show two ways to draw some text, with and without the optional arguments. The results are shown in Figure 2.13.

```
>>> from turtle import *
>>> reset()
>>> write("Python is way cool!")
>>> up()
>>> goto(0, 60)
 >>> write("Python is way cool!", move = True, align = "Center",
         font = ("Arial", 14, "bold"))
```

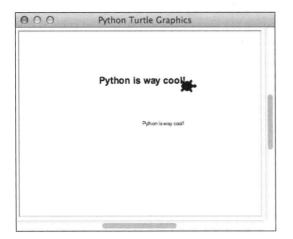

Figure 2.13
Drawing text.
© 2014 Python Software Foundation.

Note that the default alignment is left, the turtle does not move, and the text font is quite small. A font is expressed as a tuple, which contains the font name, point size, and style. Note also that if the turtle moves, it draws a line under the text. To avoid this effect, pick up the turtle before calling `write`.

USING THE TURTLE'S WINDOW AND CANVAS

The turtle graphics window provides a partial view of a canvas or drawing area that lies beneath it. If the turtle moves beyond this visible area, you can either enlarge the window or scroll to the area of the canvas that you want to view.

The canvas is initially 400 pixels wide by 300 pixels high. The function `screensize` returns the current dimensions of the canvas. When you supply the first two optional arguments to this function, it resets the width and height of the canvas to these integers. An optional third argument is a color value for the background color.

The window's initial width is 50% of your screen's width and 75% of its height. The window is centered on your screen. The functions window_width and window_height return the window's current width and height, respectively. (Recall that the user may alter these dimensions with the mouse at any time.)

To change the size and position of the window under program control, call the setup function. The first two arguments to set up are the window's dimensions. If these arguments are integers, they represent the actual width and height. If these arguments are floating-point numbers, they represent fractions of the screen's width and height. The third and fourth arguments represent the window's position relative to the boundaries of the screen. If these arguments are positive, they indicate the distances of the window from the left boundary and the top boundary, respectively. If they are negative, the distances are relative to the right and bottom edges of the screen.

The next shell session places a turtle graphics window in the upper-right corner of the screen. The background color is black, and the pen and fill colors are white.

```
>>> setup(400, 300, -400, 50)
>>> screensize(1650, 1080, "black")
>>> color("white", "white")
```

Table 2.7 summarizes the functions related to the window and canvas in turtle graphics.

Table 2.7   Functions Related to the Window and Canvas

Function	What It Does
screensize()	Returns the tuple (canvasWidth, canvasHeight).
screensize(canvwidth, canvheight, bg)	Sets the width, height, and background color of the canvas. (All arguments are optional.)
setup(width, height, startx, starty)	Sets the size and position of the turtle graphics window. width and height can be integers (the actual number of pixels) or floats (the percentages of the screen's dimensions). startx and starty can be positive (the position in pixels from the left edge of the screen) or negative (the position in pixels from the right edge of the screen).
window_height()	Returns the height of the turtle graphics window.
window_width()	Returns the width of the turtle graphics window.

Using a Configuration File

As you become proficient with turtle graphics, you will want to customize the settings for the initial state of the turtle and its window. You can put your settings in a configuration file, so you won't have to run them in your code each time you start up IDLE.

When you import resources from the `turtle` module, Python looks for a file named `turtle.cfg` in the current working directory. This should be a text file containing your settings. If the file exists, Python automatically calls the appropriate functions with the data contained in the configuration file. Here is an example of some of the settings that Python uses by default:

```
width = 0.5
height = 0.75
leftright = None
topbottom = None
canvwidth = 400
canvheight = 300
colormode = 1.0
shape = classic
pencolor = black
fillcolor = black
title = Python Turtle Graphics
```

Note that the string values for the colors, shape, and window title are written without the quotes.

There are many other turtle graphics functions not covered in this chapter. If you're curious about them, check the documentation. Some of them handle user inputs from the keyboard and the mouse. Others are useful for programming animations. You will learn about some of these operations later in this book. For now, practice using the basic functions introduced here, before you move on to the next chapter.

Summary

- Turtle graphics supports drawing pictures with a virtual pen and canvas. You can access turtle graphics operations by running the statement `from turtle import *`.
- The turtle has a position, heading, speed, pen size, shape, pen color, and fill color. You can examine these attributes or change them by calling the appropriate functions.

■ You can show or hide the turtle, and you can pick up its pen or place it down on the canvas.

■ The turtle's position is located within a two-dimensional coordinate system whose origin (0, 0) is at the center of the canvas.

■ You can move the turtle forward or backward a given distance in its current heading.

■ You can rotate the turtle's heading to the left or the right by a given number of degrees.

■ You can examine and reset the dimensions of the turtle's canvas and window. You can examine or reset the color of the canvas.

■ The reset function restores the original state of turtle graphics, whereas the clear function just erases the turtle's drawings.

■ Colors are represented in two modes. The first mode uses names, such as "red" and "blue", for a few common colors. The second mode uses the RGB system. In this system, color values are tuples of the form (r, g, b), where each item is an integer ranging from 0 through 255. The integers represent the intensities of the red, green, and blue components of a color. There are 255^3 colors available in this mode.

■ The begin_fill and end_fill functions enclose a code segment that fills a shape with the turtle's current fill color.

■ The write function draws text in the turtle graphics window.

EXERCISES

Launch the IDLE shell and complete the following exercises. You should write your code interactively in the IDLE shell.

1. The Müller-Lyer illusion is caused by an image that consists of two parallel line segments. One line segment looks like an arrow with two heads, and the other line segment looks like an arrow with two tails. Although the line segments are the same length, they appear to be unequal (see Figure 2.14). Illustrate this illusion with turtle graphics.

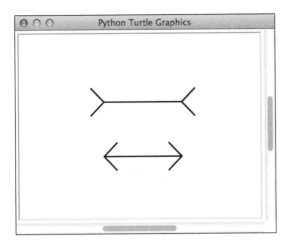

Figure 2.14
The Müller-Lyer illusion.
© 2014 Python Software Foundation.

2. Draw the following geometric shapes so they appear in the same turtle graphics window. The turtle should begin in the home position when you're drawing each shape.

   a. A square of length 40.

   b. A pentagon of length 50.

   c. A hexagon of length 60.

   d. An octagon of length 80.

CHAPTER 3

CONTROL STRUCTURES: SEQUENCING, ITERATION, AND SELECTION

In the previous chapter, you learned how to draw some simple geometric shapes, such as squares and triangles, using basic turtle graphics operations. Each basic operation models what you would do when drawing these shapes with pencil and paper; for example, turn left 90 degrees, and then move forward 70 units. When you entered a *sequence* of such operations in the Python shell, you were actually writing a *computer program*.

Many programs consist of simple sequences of operations that instruct the computer to perform one task after another, until the overall task is completed and a problem is solved. However, there are two reasons why moving forward through a simple sequence of operations is not sufficient to solve some problems:

1. The type of operation to perform might depend on some aspect of the current situation in the computer's world. For example, if you enter a bad password, the program must detect this and respond with an error message; otherwise, the program can go ahead and log you in for the requested service. This type of control, in which a choice of operations is based on a condition, is called *selection*.

2. You might need to perform a sequence of operations several times. For example, if you enter an incorrect password three times, the program might block further attempts until you contact the service by phone. This type of control, in which the same sequence of operations is repeated, is called *iteration*.

It turns out that sequencing, selection, and iteration are the only types of *control structures* really needed to solve any problem with a computer program. In this chapter, you return to the Python shell to experiment with these control structures.

REPEATING A SEQUENCE OF STATEMENTS: ITERATION

The simplest form of control structure iterates or repeats a given sequence of operations a fixed number of times. This structure, called a *definite loop*, is examined first. You will see examples of indefinite loops, which incorporate a selection component, later in this chapter.

The for Loop

When you drew a square in the last chapter, you actually entered the two expressions

```
>>> forward(70)
>>> left(90)
```

a total of four times. Wouldn't it be nice if you could just tell Python to repeat these two operations four times, instead of writing them four times yourself?

Python provides a control structure called a for loop for just this purpose. Now start up turtle graphics and enter this statement into the shell. (Remember that the >>> symbol is the shell prompt, not part of your code.)

```
>>> for count in range(4):
        forward(70)
        left(90)


>>>
```

Note that the sequence of two drawing operations appears just once and is indented in the *body* of the loop structure. The indentation is significant, in that it tells Python (and you, the reader) which statements belong to the sequence to be repeated. You end this sequence and the loop by pressing the Return or Enter key twice.

The *heading* of the loop structure, for count in range(4):, is Python's way of saying, "repeat the following sequence of operations four times." Note that Python automatically indents each statement in the sequence of statements after the loop heading.

Now compose a loop that draws a triangle. Actually, you don't have to rewrite all the code; just place the cursor at the end of the last expression in the previous loop and press Enter. This copies and pastes the code after the next shell prompt. Which parts of the code do you still have to edit to draw a triangle? Assuming that the length of a side doesn't change, you need three sides and three left turns of 120 degrees each. When you make these changes to the code and press Enter twice, you should see your triangle within the square.

Now use the same loop structure again to draw a pentagon, a hexagon, and an octagon. The result should look like your solution to Exercise 1.2 in Chapter 1, "Getting Started with Python," but your code is much easier to write.

The real power of a for loop is that it allows you to write a short sequence of statements and then repeat it any number of times that you like.

Nested Loops

Suppose that you want to draw several hexagons of the same length in different positions or orientations. For example, you might want to rotate 10 hexagons around the origin to produce the pattern shown in Figure 3.1.

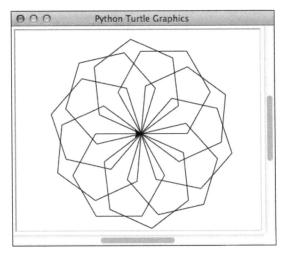

Figure 3.1
Using 10 hexagons to produce a pattern.
© 2014 Python Software Foundation.

You already know how to use a loop to draw a single hexagon. Now you want to repeat that process 10 times and adjust the heading of the turtle by 36 degrees after each hexagon is drawn. Here is a design plan for the complete process:

```
Repeat 10 times
    Draw a hexagon
    Turn left 36 degrees
```

This design plan is expressed in *pseudocode*. Pseudocode cannot be run as actual program code, but it is close enough to English and to Python that it can serve as a blueprint for writing the equivalent Python code.

Now you translate this pseudocode design to Python code. The first statement in the body of the loop expands to another loop to draw a hexagon. The entire design expands to the following Python code:

```
>>> for count in range(10):
        for count in range(6):
                forward(70)
                left(60)
        left(36)
```

In this code, the loop that draws the hexagon is nested with another loop. Note how the indentation helps you and Python determine which statements belong in the bodies of the two loops. When you enter this code into the shell, be careful to press the Delete or Backspace key once after entering the line left(60) so that the line left(36) aligns with the second line beginning with for. On each pass through the outer loop, the inner loop is run first. When the inner loop terminates, the turtle turns left 36 degrees before drawing the next hexagon.

You can vary the pattern drawn in the turtle graphics window by changing the number of iterations and the turtle's rotation angle in the outer loop or by changing the type of shape drawn by the inner loop. You are encouraged to experiment with different combinations of these options.

How the range Function Works with a for Loop

If you want to repeat a sequence of operations a given number of times, the loop patterns just shown suffice. However, you might want to iterate through a sequence of values and use each value for some purpose in the body of the loop. For example, consider computing the sum total of the integers from 1 through 10. The following code fragments accomplish this:

```
>>> total = 0
>>> for number in range(1, 11):
        total = total + number

>>> total
55
```

The for loop is set up to iterate over a sequence of values. When used with the range function, the loop iterates over each integer included in a range of integers. As you saw in Chapter 1, when range is called with a single integer argument, it produces a sequence of integers, ranging from 0 through the integer argument minus one. On each pass through the loop, the current value in the sequence is automatically assigned to the variable in the loop heading. You can use this variable in the loop body, as shown in following code fragment:

```
>>> for number in range(5):
        print(number)

>>>
0
1
2
3
4
```

You also saw that you can begin a range with a value other than 0 by calling the range function with two arguments. For example, you can print the integers from 1 through 5 by passing the arguments 1 and 6 to range.

Finally, you can visit a range of integers in descending order by calling the range function with three arguments. The first argument is the upper bound, the second argument is the lower bound minus one, and the third argument is –1.

You should experiment with all three of these methods of counting with a for loop until you understand how they work.

Loops with Strings, Lists, and Dictionaries

Because a for loop visits items in a sequence, it can also visit the items in a string or a list. The next code fragments demonstrate this:

```
>>> name = "Kenneth"
>>> for ch in name:
        print(ch)
```

K
e
n
n
e
t
h

```
>>> fruits = ["banana", "apple", "orange"]
>>> for fruit in fruits:
        print(fruit)


banana
apple
orange
>>>
```

Although dictionaries are not sequences, when you supply a dictionary to a `for` loop, the loop visits the dictionary's keys in some unspecified order. For example, to display a dictionary's keys and their values, you might run the following code:

```
>>> kenInfo = {"name":"Ken", "hair-color":"gray", "age":63}
>>> for key in kenInfo:
        print(key, kenInfo[key])


name Ken
age 63
hair-color gray
>>>
```

As you can see, the `for` loop is easy to use as long as you have a sequence of items to process or a definite number of iterations to perform.

ASKING QUESTIONS: BOOLEAN EXPRESSIONS

As mentioned earlier, a computer program may have to respond to conditions in the computer's environment to select which course of action to take. Examining these conditions takes the form of asking yes/no questions. For example, is the integer value greater than 0? Is the turtle at the right edge of the turtle graphics window? Does the file exist in the current working directory? Is the length of the list equal to 0? These questions take the form of Boolean expressions in Python code. In this section, you explore various ways of getting answers to yes/no questions with Boolean expressions.

Boolean Values

Named for the nineteenth century British mathematician and logician George Boole, a Boolean expression returns one of two values: True or False. These values are taken to mean "yes" or "no" when they result from evaluating Boolean expressions. Like the words for, from, and import, the words True and False are Python *keywords*. They are colored orange in IDLE and cannot be used as the names of variables. Like the numbers and other literals, the values True and False evaluate to themselves.

Comparisons

The == operator compares any two Python values for equality and returns True if they're equal and False if they're not. The != operator stands for "not equal to" and returns the opposite results of ==. Here are some example comparisons:

```
>>> 34 == 0
False
>>> 34 != 0
True
>>> 34 == 2 * 17
True
>>> "Ken" == "KEN"
False
>>> "Ken" == 34
False
```

As you can see, comparisons are Boolean expressions. Note that Python compares two strings by examining the pairs of characters at each position. Because "e" does not equal "E", the strings "Ken" and "KEN" are not equal.

The operators <, >, <=, and >= are used to compare values that can be ordered in ascending or descending order. Thus, you can compare two numbers or two strings in this manner. You should try these other comparison operators in the shell to make sure you understand their meanings.

Logical Operations

Boole used the values True and False in a system of logic. There are three basic operations in this system:

- **Logical negation**—This operation applies the logical operator not to a Boolean expression. The result returned is False if the expression is True and True if the expression is False.

- **Logical conjunction**—This operation applies the logical operator and to two operands, both of which are Boolean expressions. The operation returns True if both of the expressions are True, and it returns False otherwise.

- **Logical disjunction**—This operation applies the logical operator or to two operands, both of which are Boolean expressions. The operation returns False if both of the expressions are False; otherwise, it returns True.

Suppose that a program receives an input number from the user, and you want to test it to verify that its value is within a range of values, say, from 0 through 100. For this condition to be True, the number must be greater than or equal to 0 and less than or equal to 100. The following shell session shows some tests for this condition:

```
>>> number = int(input("Enter a number: "))
Enter a number: 55
>>> number >= 0 and number <= 100
True
>>> number = int(input("Enter a number: "))
Enter a number: -1
>>> number >= 0 and number <= 100
False
>>> number = int(input("Enter a number: "))
Enter a number: 101
>>> number >= 0 and number <= 100
False
```

Logical operations might seem strange at first, but they are actually easier to understand than arithmetic operations once you get used to them. The main reason for this is that there is only a finite number of possible combinations of values for the operands. You can list these combinations and the results in *truth tables*. Table 3.1 shows the combinations and results for negation. Table 3.2 shows the combinations and results for conjunction and disjunction. Note that both A and B refer to Boolean expressions.

Table 3.1   The Truth Table for Logical Negation

A	not A
True	False
False	True

A	B	A and B	A or B
True	True	True	True
True	False	False	True
False	True	False	True
False	False	False	False

Table 3.2 The Truth Table for Logical Conjunction and Logical Disjunction

You probably won't use logical operations very often. But if you need help with them, you can always review these tables for their evaluation rules and then try your expressions in the shell.

MAKING CHOICES: SELECTION STATEMENTS

After you determine how to ask a yes/no question about a condition, you must decide what to do with the answer. Sometimes you take action if the answer is "yes" but do nothing if it is "no." For example, if the remainder of an integer division is not 0, you would output the remainder; otherwise, the output of the quotient, which happened earlier, would suffice.

Other times, you perform one action if the answer to your question is "yes" but another action if the answer is "no." For example, if a password is recognized, you can perform the requested service; otherwise, you output an error message to the user.

Still other times, there may be many different options available, but only one of them is input. You must compare the input to each possible option until a match is found, whereupon you perform the associated action. Command menus call for this type of multiway decision.

In this section, you explore Python's different types of selection statements for making one-way, two-way, and multiway decisions.

The One-Way if Statement

You use the one-way if statement to make a one-way decision. Its form is

```
if BooleanExpression:
    Statements
```

where *Statements* is a sequence of one or more statements. Note the indentation before the nested statements. As in the for loop, the indentation in an if statement is significant. It picks out the statements that are run if the Boolean expression is True. If the Boolean expression is False, these statements are skipped, and the computation continues following the entire if statement. Figure 3.2 shows the flow of control in this type of selection statement.

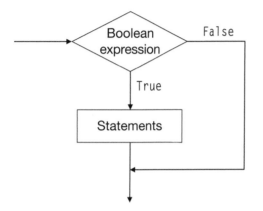

Figure 3.2
The flow of control in a one-way if statement.

Here is the example of integer division mentioned earlier:

```
>>> divisor = 10
>>> divisor = 3
>>> dividend = 10
>>> quotient = dividend // divisor
>>> remainder = dividend % divisor
>>> print("The quotient is", quotient)
The quotient is 3
>>> if remainder != 0:
        print("The remainder is", remainder)


The remainder is 1
```

As you can see, if the divisor had been 2 or the dividend had been 9, the remainder, 0, would not have been output at all.

One-way if statements are rare, but you should experiment with one just in case you have a need for it some day.

The Two-Way if Statement

Two-way decisions, like forks in the road, are common. You go one way or the other, depending on the condition you examine at the choice point. The form for a two-way if statement to make this type of choice is

```
if BooleanExpression:
    ConsequentStatements
else:
    AlternativeStatements
```

Once again, the indentation of the nested statements reflects the logic of this control structure. If the Boolean expression is True, run the consequent statements and then skip to the end of the entire if-else statement. Otherwise, skip the consequent statements and run the alternative statements following the keyword else. Figure 3.3 shows the flow of control in this type of selection statement.

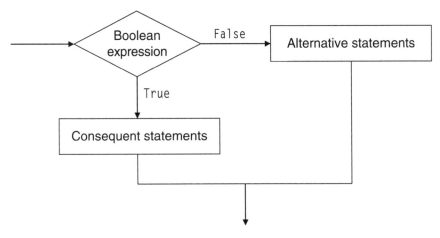

Figure 3.3
The flow of control in a two-way if statement.

Here is an example of how you can use an if-else statement to accept or reject a user's input number:

```
>>> import math
>>> number = input("Enter a positive number: ")
>>> if number > 0:
        print("The square root is", math.sqrt(number))
    else:
        print("Error: the number must be greater than 0")
```

Probable Options with random.randint

In Chapter 1, you saw how to use Python's `random.choice` function with a list to simulate a coin toss:

```
>>> import random
>>> coin = ["heads", "tails"]
>>> random.choice(coin)
'tails'
```

Because there are two options from which to choose, picking one at random causes each option to be chosen approximately 50% of the time over the course of many tosses. To demonstrate this, you can run the following code fragments, which count the number of heads and tails over 50 tosses:

```
>>> headCount = 0
>>> tailCount = 0
>>> for count in range(50):
        result = (random.choice(coin))
        if result == "heads":
                headCount += 1
        else:
                tailCount += 1


>>> headCount
22
>>> tailCount
28
```

As you can see, over the long haul, a coin toss turns up heads about half of the time and tails about half of the time. In mathematical terms, each side of the coin turns up with a probability of .5. As a rule, if an event has a probability of 1, it means that it is certain to occur (100% of the time). Smaller probability values correlate to smaller percentages.

Occasionally, you will want to select an option based on a given probability value. Suppose that the probability of that option is .25 (1 out of 4). Instead of building a Python list of four values, you can pick a random integer from a range of integers using the function `random.randint`. This function expects two arguments: the lower and upper bounds of the range. Thus, to select an option with a probability of .25, you can call `random.randint(1, 4)` and compare the result to a given number, say, 1. Over the long haul, you should see this number returned 25% of the time, as shown in the next shell session:

```
>>> total = 0
>>> for count in range(50):
        result = random.randint(1, 4)
        if result == 1:
                total += 1


>>> total
13
>>> 4 * 13
52
```

This method works well for probabilities expressed as the fractions ½, ¼, and so forth, but what about fractions with larger numerators, such as ¾? This means that you are looking for any of 3 given numbers out of 4. Expressed in English, you want to see if a random number between 1 and 4 is in the range from 1 to 3. Here is the Python code for this test:

```
>>> random.randint(1, 4) in range(1, 4)
False
```

To verify that this expression returns True three-quarters of the time, test it in loop like the others shown in this section.

Using these techniques, you should be able to perform an action in code with any given probability that is required by a problem. The exercises give you a chance to perform further experiments with probability.

The Multiway if Statement

You must make a multiway decision when there are more than two possible paths of action. (Most conventional forks have four prongs, after all.) Thus, there are at least two conditions that must be checked in this kind of situation. Python provides a multiway if statement for this purpose. Its form is

```
if BooleanExpression:
    statements
elif Booleanexpression:
    statements
.

.
else:
    statements
```

After you ask the first question in the `if` clause, you can ask as many questions with `elif` clauses as you need to. The trailing `else` clause, which is optional, handles the case where the answer to all the questions is `False`, or "no." Note that only one sequence of statements is chosen and run.

The following code fragments demonstrate a simple command interpreter for doing arithmetic:

```
>>> x = float(input("Enter the first number: "))
Enter the first number: 3.44
>>> y = float(input("Enter the second number: "))
Enter the second number: 45.6
>>> command = input("Enter an arithmetic operator [+, -, *, /]: ")
Enter an arithmetic operator [+, -, *, /]: *
>>> if command == "+":
        print("The sum is", x + y)
elif command == "-":
        print("The differnce is", x - y)
elif command == "*":
        print("The product is", x * y)
elif command == "/":
        print("The quotient is", x / y)
else:
        print("Error: unrecognized operator")
The product is 156.864
```

You will see uses of selection statements in turtle graphics programs later in this chapter.

Using Selection to Control Iteration

The `for` loop examined earlier is quite rigid. It iterates a definite number of times, over some fixed sequence of values. This type of loop is simple to design and works well for many problems. However, some situations call for a more flexible type of loop: one that cannot anticipate how many iterations will be performed. This type of loop must be able to ask the question, "Should I continue or not?" and be able to exit when the answer is "no." This type of loop is called an *indefinite loop*, and in this section, you explore how to design indefinite loops for various situations.

The while Loop

Python provides a control structure called a while loop for when you can't predict how many times the loop will iterate. Its form is quite simple:

```
while BooleanExpression:
    Statements
```

This form looks a bit like that of the one-way if statement discussed earlier. The behavior is similar, too. The difference is that the loop repeatedly tests the Boolean expression until it becomes False. Whenever the expression returns True, the statements in the body of the loop are run; otherwise, the body of the loop is skipped, and computation continues after the loop. Thus, the statements in the one-way if statement are run once or not at all, whereas the statements in the while loop are run zero or more times. Figure 3.4 shows the flow of control in this type of loop.

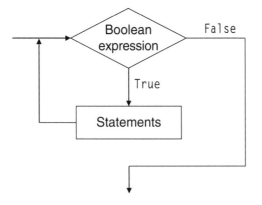

Figure 3.4
The flow of control in a while loop.

A while loop can be used like a for loop, to move through a sequence of values, as shown in the next shell session:

```
>>> number = 0
>>> while number < 5:
        print(number)
        number = number + 1

>>>
0
1
2
3
4
```

However, the `while` loop really comes into its own when the number of iterations is unpredictable. For example, consider Euclid's method for computing the greatest common divisor of two integers. The greatest common divisor of two integers is the largest integer by which both numbers can be evenly divided (with a remainder of 0). For instance, the greatest common divisor of 120 and 32 is 8. Euclid's method starts with the two numbers A and B and assumes A >= B and B >= 0. You repeatedly replace B with the remainder of dividing A by B and replace A with B. You stop when B equals 0; at that point, A is the answer. Here is a pseudocode design for this method:

```
While B > 0
    C = A remainder B
    A = B
    B = C
```

When A = 128 and B = 32, the loop sets A to 32 and B to 24 on the first pass. On the second pass, A becomes 24 and B becomes 8. On the third and final pass, A becomes 8 and B becomes 0. You can confirm that this is how Euclid's method works with Python code in the following shell session:

```
>>> a = 120
>>> b = 32
>>> while b > 0:
        c = a % b
        a = b
        b = c
        print(a, b)


32 24
24 8
8 0
>>> a
8
```

As you can see, it's impossible to anticipate the number of iterations required for any given values of A and B. Therefore, the `while` loop is the appropriate loop control structure to use for Euclid's method.

Random Walks in Turtle Graphics

In the turtle graphics examples seen thus far, your turtle has moved in quite rigid and regular ways to draw geometric shapes. But consider the movements of animals, such as insects, in their natural environment. Their movements might be determined by the near-ness of food or potential predators. Other movements might appear to be quite random; they seem to just wander around.

To simulate this type of random movement, you can make the turtle take a *random walk*. One way to do this is to move the turtle a random distance and then turn a random num-ber of degrees to the left or right. You repeat this process a given number of times. You use Python's function `random.randint` to obtain a random integer within a given range. The following shell session produces the random walk shown in Figure 3.5.

```
>>> from random import randint
>>> reset()
>>> for count in range(30):
        distance = randint(10, 60)
        forward(distance)
        degrees = randint(45, 135)
        if randint(1, 2) == 1:
                left(degrees)
        else:
                right(degrees)
```

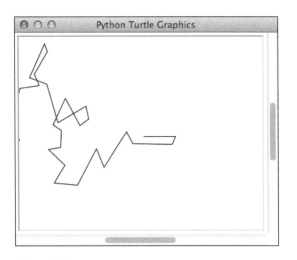

Figure 3.5
A random walk.
© 2014 Python Software Foundation.

Note that the turtle might walk beneath the edge of the window for a bit and then return to the visible area of the canvas.

A more interesting scenario has the turtle stopping when it encounters a piece of food or an obstacle that it can't get around. This type of process calls for an indefinite loop that continues while such an encounter has not occurred. The next shell session directs the turtle to move around until it encounters one of the edges of its window. Figure 3.6 shows a result.

```
>>> reset()
>>> width = window_width()
>>> height = window_height()
>>> (minX, maxX) = (-(width / 2), width / 2)
>>> (minY, maxY) = (-(height / 2), height / 2)
>>> (x, y) = position()
>>> while x > minX and y > minY and x < maxX and y < maxY:
        distance = randint(10, 60)
        forward(distance)
        degrees = randint(45, 135)
        if randint(1, 2) == 1:
                left(degrees)
        else:
                right(degrees)
        (x, y) = position()
```

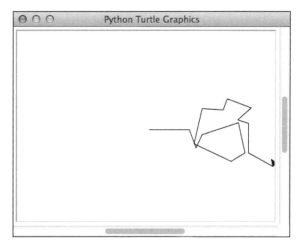

Figure 3.6
A random walk to a boundary.

Because the distances and headings are random, and the user may alter the size of the window at runtime, the number of paths that the turtle takes on any given walk is unpredictable. That's why you must use a `while` loop in this case.

SUMMARY

- The basic control structures in programming are sequencing, selection, and iteration.

- A sequence of statements consists of one statement written after another. The computer runs them in the order in which they appear.

- A selection statement tests at least one condition. If the condition is `True`, the computer runs the sequence of statements. Otherwise, the computer skips this sequence and runs the code following it.

- A one-way `if` statement contains one test of a condition, followed by a sequence of statements. A two-way `if` statement contains one test of a condition, followed by two alternative sequences of statements. A multiway `if` statement contains two or more tests of conditions, each of which is followed by an alternative sequence of statements.

- The two Boolean values are `True` and `False`.

- A condition is a Boolean expression. A Boolean expression returns `True` or `False`.

- The comparison operators ==, !=, <, >, <=, and >= can compare integers, floating-point numbers, or strings. Comparisons return `True` or `False`.

- The logical operators `and`, `or`, and `not` take Boolean expressions as operands. Logical operations return `True` or `False`.

- The rules for logical operations are described in truth tables.

- A `for` loop is used to repeat a sequence of statements a definite number of times.

- A `for` loop uses the `range` function to count through a sequence of integers.

- A `for` loop can visit the characters in a string, the items in a list or tuple, and the keys in a dictionary.

- A `while` loop is used to repeat a sequence of statements zero or more times. The loop is governed by the test of a condition, which must be `True` for the loop to continue running the sequence of statements.

EXERCISES

Launch the IDLE shell and complete the following exercises. You should write your code interactively in the IDLE shell.

1. You have drawn various geometric shapes by moving the turtle forward and then turning left. Write a code fragment that draws a circle in a similar manner. Hint: the turtle turns 1 degree to the left. How do you increase or decrease the size of your circles?

2. You can modify your code from Exercise 1 to draw a spiral. Start by calling `left` with a larger number of degrees, say, 4, and observe what happens. Then clear the drawing and set a new variable named `distance` to 1. Use this variable as the argument to move forward within the loop, and increment the variable by a small amount, say, .05, on each pass through the loop. How do you increase or decrease the number of rotations and the distance between them?

CHAPTER 4

COMPOSING, SAVING, AND RUNNING PROGRAMS

Thus far in this book, you have been entering short Python code fragments into the IDLE shell and viewing the results. This method works well for experimenting with the basic elements of Python, including the turtle graphics operations. However, as the things you want to do with your code get more complicated, so does your code. At that point, entering lots of small pieces of code into the shell becomes unwieldy and inconvenient. When you put related code fragments together, you really have what counts as a *computer program*. What you need now is an editor for composing programs, a means of saving them to files for later use, and a means of running them. The programming process and its supporting tools are the topics of this chapter.

EXPLORING THE PROGRAM DEVELOPMENT PROCESS

A *program* is a sequence of statements or instructions that solves a problem. Programs can be as short as a single line of code or can consist of millions of lines of code. Software companies may employ many teams of programmers to work on a single large program. Each team is responsible for working on a solution to a piece of the overall problem (for example, the spell checker, file manager, and editor in a word processing program). Each team in turn may be composed of smaller teams who work on different stages of the programming process. These stages include the following, which are also shown in the flow diagram of Figure 4.1:

1. **Analysis**—In this stage, you determine exactly what counts as a solution to a problem. For example, a spell checker should check the spelling of words in a text file

and make changes where necessary. Note that you do no coding here, but you determine what the results of your program should be. You will check the program for these results during program testing. You might also write the manual for the program's users.

2. **Design**—In this stage, you use the results of analysis to determine how the program will solve its assigned problem. Some coding might occur here, although design tools such as the pseudocode that you saw in Chapter 3, "Control Structures: Sequencing, Iteration, and Selection," might also be used.

3. **Coding**—In this stage, you translate the results of design into the code of a programming language. Note that the same design could be coded in different languages, such as Python, Java, and C++, depending on the needs of the client and the computer system where the program will be run.

4. **Compilation**—In this stage, you run a program that translates your program into a form that can be run on a computer. Compilation may reveal syntax errors, which you must correct before continuing.

5. **Testing**—In this stage, you repeatedly run the program with different inputs and observe the outputs. If the program halts with an error message, or if the program produces unexpected outputs, you have to retreat to an earlier phase to fix the errors.

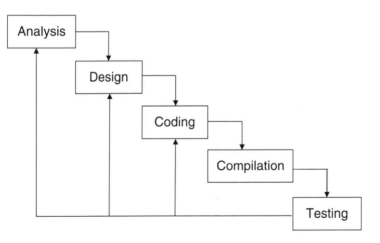

Figure 4.1
The program development process.

Very rarely would you participate in all of these stages in a large programming project. In fact, you might have an entire career in just one area, as an analyst, designer, coder, or tester. But for short programs, you might do everything.

Throughout this book, you will conduct analysis, design, and testing informally. In this chapter, you will focus on the tools in IDLE for coding, compiling, and running Python programs.

COMPOSING A PROGRAM

Thus far in this book, you have typed your Python code fragments in the IDLE shell and run them there. You have viewed the results either in the shell window or in a turtle graphics window. When you want to enter and save code that you can edit and run later, you can open a new file in IDLE and work in a separate window. In this section, you learn how to do that. You also explore the kind of structure your code should have, as a complete Python program.

Program Edits

There are several ways to edit a program with IDLE. Each one depends on where you are in the process.

- You're starting from scratch on a new program. You launch IDLE and then select the New File option from the shell window's File menu. A new, empty window pops up. You can then place the two windows (the shell and the file windows) side by side on your screen and get to work.

- You've been experimenting with code fragments in the shell, and you want to write a complete program. You just open a new file window as before.

- You want to edit a file that you saved earlier or that you got from another programmer. You launch IDLE and select the Open option from the File menu. You then browse for the file in your file system. On some systems, such as Mac OS, you can combine both of these steps into one by launching (double-clicking on) the Python program file in its directory window. Finally, you can run the command `idle3 filename` in a terminal window after navigating to the file's directory with the appropriate system commands in the terminal window.

Like a word processor, IDLE lets you have several file windows open at the same time. Thus, you could open windows on existing program files to copy code from them to a new program in a different window. Note that your Python code in these windows is color-coded, just as it is in the shell window. IDLE also knows how to indent your code automatically when you enter selection statements and loops. Common editing commands, such as Copy/Cut/Paste and Find/Replace, are similar to those of the word processors on your particular system. The Format menu includes some commands for formatting Python code and cleaning up indentation problems.

To save a program to a file, select the Save option from the File menu, or use the control key sequence on your particular system (Command+S on a Mac, and Ctrl+S on other systems). Python program files have a .py extension. If you don't provide that when you save a file for the first time, Python adds it for you.

Program Structure

As you saw in Chapter 3, some Python statements, such as loops and selection statements, have a structure. Python follows this structure to run the statements, just as you follow it to understand what they mean.

A complete Python program also has a structure—one that you employ in each program you write. Here is an example turtle graphics program that draws a pattern of hexagon shapes similar to the one you saw in Chapter 3. You can find this program in the file named samplepattern.py on the companion website (www.cengageptr.com/downloads). The next few subsections explain each part of the program's structure.

```python
"""
samplepattern.py
Draws a pattern using a hexagon.
"""

from turtle import *

def main():
    reset()
    speed(0)
    pensize(2)
    hideturtle()
    color("blue", "yellow")     # Blue outline, yellow fill
    begin_fill()
    for count in range(10):     # Draw 10 hexagons
        for count in range(6):  # Draw each hexagon
            forward(70)
            left(60)
        left(36)                # Rotate them evenly
    end_fill()
    return "Done!"
```

```
if __name__ == '__main__':
    msg = main()
    print(msg)
    mainloop()
```

Docstrings and End-of-Line Comments

The first four lines at the top of this program form a string enclosed in triple-double quotes. When a string appears in Python code in this manner, it is called a *docstring*. Python ignores docstrings when it runs a program, but you should not ignore docstrings when you read it. This docstring tells you the name of the program's file and summarizes what the program does. Python also displays a program's docstrings when you ask for help with the help function in the shell. Although the docstring in this program seems to provide only trivial information, it's a good idea to make a practice of beginning all of your programs with docstrings.

About halfway into the program code, you see several pieces of text that begin with the # character and are colored red in IDLE. Python also ignores this text, called *end-of-line comments*, at runtime. Once again, this information is there for you, the reader, to help you understand what's going on at those points in the program code. You should include end-of-line comments sparingly—only when you think your code needs some clarification.

import Statements

This program uses turtle graphics functions, so it must import them, as you did in your shell experimentation. In a program file, all import statements should appear before the rest of the program code. Note that blank lines, which Python ignores, separate the initial docstring from the import section and that section from the rest of the program code.

The main Function

Although Python does not require it, programmers typically organize their top-level code in a main function. The next part of the example program defines this function, which is not built in to Python. Note that the function's first line, or *heading*, is aligned to the left of its code, or *body*, by indentation. The body of the main function contains the sequence of statements that are run when the function is called. That's all you need to know about function definitions for now.

Review the code in the main function. It sets up the initial state of the turtle so that it can draw the pattern of hexagons, and then it runs the nested for loop to do so. When the main function has finished its work, it returns the string "Done!" to its caller with a return statement.

Each turtle graphics program that you write from now on will contain a main function. You can use this first one as a template and just edit the code before the return statement.

The if main == "__main__" Idiom

The last four lines of code in the program form a one-way if statement. This statement determines whether the code is being run as a Python program or whether it is being imported as a Python module. Once again, Python does not require this part, but it is standard practice for Python programmers.

Each Python program file can be viewed as a *module*. Which view Python takes of a file depends on how it's loaded into the Python runtime system. If you were to enter the statement import samplepattern into the shell, Python would view the file as a module. You could then get help by entering help(samplepattern) or call the main function by entering samplepattern.main(). The next shell session shows the results of entering the first two commands:

```
>>> import samplepattern
>>> help(samplepattern)
Help on module samplepattern:

NAME
    samplepattern

DESCRIPTION
    samplepattern.py
    Draws a pattern using a hexagon.

FUNCTIONS
    main()

FILE
    /Users/ken/examples/samplepattern.py
```

However, if you were to run the program from an IDLE file window or from a terminal window (as described in the next section), the program itself would have to call its own main function to start things up. That's the purpose of the one-way if statement at the end of the program.

When the program is imported as a module, Python sets the hidden *module variable* __main__ to the name of the module—in this case, "samplepattern". But if the program is launched from an IDLE file window or from a terminal window, Python gives this variable the value "__main__". So you can see that the logic of the one-way if statement makes the right thing happen, no matter what. If __name__ is "__main__", the program calls the main function to run the program. Otherwise, the program does nothing further but has already loaded the other pieces of code that belong to this module.

The mainloop Function

Now it's time to look more closely at the last three lines of code in the example program. The first line calls the main function, which pops up the turtle graphics window and draws the pattern. At that point, main returns the string "Done!" The program then outputs this string either to the IDLE shell or to the terminal window, depending on the launch method. The last line of code calls the mainloop() function. This function causes the turtle graphics window to stay open when the program is run from a terminal window. If you are running the program from an IDLE file window, you cannot return to the shell until you close the turtle graphics window.

RUNNING A PROGRAM

By now you will be eager to run the example program. This section explores a couple of ways to do this. But first you need a quick reminder about using a turtle graphics configuration file.

Using a Turtle Graphics Configuration File

As mentioned in Chapter 2, "Getting Started with Turtle Graphics," a turtle graphics configuration file can provide the same initial settings for several programs. For example, you might want a smaller initial turtle graphics window and the full RGB color mode. Many of the example programs in the rest of this book use a configuration file with the following settings:

```
width = 400
height = 300
canvwidth = 1200
canvheight = 900
using_IDLE = True
colormode = 255
title = Python Turtle Graphics
```

This file is named turtle.cfg and should sit in the same directory as your Python program file. Of course, you are free to modify any of these settings from within your program after it launches.

Running a Program from an IDLE Window

Now, at long last, you are ready to run a Python program. The easiest way to do so in IDLE is to place your mouse cursor in the program file window and press the Function +5 or F5 key. If the program has not yet been saved, Python stops you with a request to do that. Then, if the program has not yet been compiled, Python does that. If there are no syntax errors, Python loads the resulting code into its runtime system and runs the program. In the case of the example program, you should now see three windows: the shell window, the file window, and the turtle graphics window, as shown in Figure 4.2.

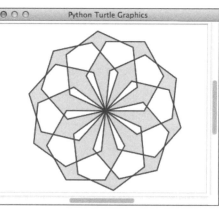

Figure 4.2
Running a program in IDLE.
© 2014 Python Software Foundation.

Note that if there are any runtime errors in the program (but there should be none in this example), the error messages appear in red, as always, in the shell window.

To quit your running program, close the turtle graphics window. At that point, control returns to the shell, and you can make any desired changes to the program in the file window.

When you develop programs in the rest of this book, you'll be working with windows of this sort in IDLE. Learn where the F5 key is!

Running a Program from a Terminal Window

If you want to give a finished Python program to others, note that they will likely run it from a terminal window. To try this yourself, open a terminal window and navigate to the directory that contains the file samplepattern.py. Then enter the command

```
python3 samplepattern.py
```

in the terminal window. The turtle graphics window should pop up and display the pattern. When you close this window, the program quits and returns control to the terminal window. Note that the message "Done!" should be displayed in that window. If you don't want extra output like this from your program, you can delete the output statement in the penultimate line of code.

Most computer systems provide a way to set the action that is triggered when you launch a file by double-clicking on its icon. In Windows systems, this action runs the Python program. In Mac OS, this action opens an IDLE file window. Also, in either system, you must make sure that Python 3.0 or higher is installed.

Using the sys Module and Command-Line Arguments

When you run a program from a terminal window, you can usually provide optional *command-line arguments*. For example, the idle3 command pops up a shell window, but you can instead run idle3 *filename* to open a file window. Likewise, when you run python3 *filename*, you are launching a Python program, but when you run just python3, a shell opens (in the terminal window itself, not in an IDLE window).

Python lets you distribute programs that you can run with additional command-line arguments. For example, suppose you want the example program that draws a pattern with hexagons to use pentagons or octagons instead. Your program could accept an additional command-line argument that represents the number of sides in the figure. The default number would still be 6 if the user does not supply the extra argument. Here are three examples of how to use this feature in the terminal window:

```
Madison:~ ken$ python3 samplepattern.py
Done!
Madison:~ ken$ python3 samplepattern.py 5
Done!
Madison:~ ken$ python3 samplepattern.py 8
Done!
```

When a Python program is run in the terminal window, the system places each optional argument in a list of strings. The first string in this list is the program's filename. To access this list in your Python program, you import the sys module. The variable sys.argv is the name of the list.

To experiment with command-line arguments before you actually use them, try printing them at the beginning of the main function. Here are the changes to the example program to accomplish this, followed by the terminal outputs:

```
"""
samplepattern.py
Draws a pattern using a hexagon.
"""

from turtle import *
import sys

def main():
    print(sys.argv)
# The rest of the program would go here
```

Program output from two runs:

```
Madison:~ ken$ python3 samplepattern.py
['samplepattern']
Done!
Madison:~ ken$ python3 samplepattern.py 5
['samplepattern', '5']
Done!
```

Now you'll modify the program so that it handles the extra command-line argument, if there is one. Here is the relevant code, followed by an explanation.

```
from turtle import *
import sys

def main():
    if len(sys.argv) == 2:
        numSides = int(sys.argv[1])
        if numSides < 3:
            return "Error: number of sides must be > 2"
    else:
        numSides = 6
    angle = 360 / numSides               # Compute interior angle for polygon
    reset()
    speed(0)
    width(2)
    hideturtle()
    color("blue", "yellow")              # Blue outline, yellow fill
    begin_fill()
    for count in range(10):              # Draw 10 polygons
        for count in range(numSides):    # Draw each polygon
            forward(70)
            left(angle)
        left(36)                         # Rotate them evenly
    end_fill()
    return "Done!"
```

The main function now uses the variable numSides to refer to the number of sides in the shape, and it uses the variable angle to refer to the interior angle between sides in the shape. Note how these variables are initialized and then used in the loop.

The rest of the new code at the beginning of main deals with the possibility of the extra command-line argument. If the extra command-line argument is not present, the number of sides in the figure is 6, as before. Otherwise, this argument is converted to an int and checked for an error before being used to establish the number of sides and the angle.

Note the use of the nested if and return statements to handle the error.

Looking Behind the Scenes: How Python Runs Programs

Whether you are running Python code as a program or interactively in a shell, Python does a great deal of work to carry out the instructions in your program. Think for a moment about bridging the huge gap between the instructions that you write in Python code and the computer hardware that carries out these instructions. It's a gap that most programmers (and most other users of computers) never have to worry about; they all just take for granted that the programs they build or use will accomplish their tasks on any computer.

In this section, you learn a bit about what goes on underneath the hood to allow a physical device like a computer to carry out the instructions you write in Python code.

Computer Hardware

The basic hardware components of a computer are *memory*, a *central processing unit* (CPU), and a set of *input/output devices*, as shown schematically in Figure 4.3.

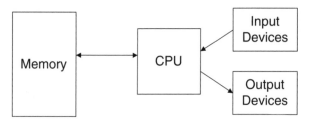

Figure 4.3
Hardware components of a modern computer system.

Human beings primarily interact with input and output devices. The input devices include a touchscreen, a keyboard, a mouse, a camera, and a microphone. Common output devices include a monitor, a printer, and speakers. Computers can also communicate with the external world through various ports that connect them to networks and to other devices such as handheld music players, digital cameras, and drone robots. The purpose of most of the input devices is to convert information that human beings deal with, such as text, images, and sounds, into information for computational processing. The purpose of most output devices is to convert the results of this processing back to human-usable form.

Computer memory is set up to represent and store information in electronic form. Specifically, information is stored as patterns of binary digits (1s and 0s), also called *bits*. To understand how this works, consider a basic device such as a non-dimming light switch, which can only be in one of two states: on or off. Now suppose there is a bank of switches that controls 16 small lights in a row. By turning the switches off or on, you can represent any pattern of 16 binary digits as patterns of lights that are on or off. Computer scientists have discovered how to represent any information, including text, images, and sound, in binary form.

Now, suppose there are 4 of these groups of 16 lights. You can select any group of lights and examine or change the state of each light within that collection. You have just developed a tiny model of computer memory. This memory has 4 cells, each of which can store 16 bits of binary information. A diagram of this model, in which the memory cells are filled with binary digits, is shown in Figure 4.4. This memory is also sometimes called *primary* or *internal* or *random access memory* (RAM).

0	1	0	1	0	1	1	1	0	1	0	0	1	1	0	1
0	1	0	0	1	1	1	1	0	1	0	1	1	0	1	0
1	1	0	1	1	1	1	1	0	1	0	0	1	1	1	1
0	1	0	0	1	0	1	1	0	1	0	1	1	0	1	1

Figure 4.4
A model of computer memory.

The information stored in memory can represent any type of data, such as numbers, text, images, sound, or the instructions of a program. You can also store in memory a program encoded as binary instructions for the computer. Once the information is stored in memory, you typically want to do something with it—that is, you want to process it. The part of a computer that is responsible for processing data is the *central processing unit* (CPU). This device, which is also sometimes called a *processor*, consists of electronic switches arranged to perform simple logical, arithmetic, and control operations. The CPU runs a machine language program by fetching its binary instructions from memory, decoding them, and executing them. Executing an instruction might involve fetching other binary information—the data—from memory as well.

The processor can quickly locate data in a computer's primary memory. However, these data exist only as long as electric power comes into the computer. If the battery fails or the power is turned off, the data in primary memory are lost. Clearly, a more permanent type of memory is needed to preserve data. This more permanent type of memory is called *external* or *secondary memory*, and it comes in several forms. Magnetic storage media, such as tapes and hard disks, allow bit patterns to be stored as patterns on a magnetic field. Semiconductor storage media, such as flash memory sticks, perform much the same function with a different technology, as do optical storage media, such as CDs and DVDs. Some of these secondary storage media can hold much larger quantities of information than the internal memory of a computer. Smartphones, tablets, and many laptops now use built-in flash memory for secondary storage as well as primary storage.

Computer Software

A computer is a general-purpose problem-solving machine. To solve any computable problem, a computer must be capable of running any program. Because it is impossible to anticipate all the problems for which there are computable solutions, there is no way to "hard-wire" all potential programs into a computer's hardware. Instead, you build some basic operations into the hardware's processor and require any program to use them. The programs are converted to binary form and then loaded, with their data, into the computer's memory. The processor can then execute the programs' instructions by running the hardware's more basic operations.

Any programs that are stored in memory so that they can be run later are called *software*. A program stored in computer memory must be represented in binary digits, also known as *machine code*. Loading machine code into computer memory one digit at a time would be a tedious, error-prone task for human beings. It would be convenient if you could automate this process to get it right every time. For this reason, computer scientists have developed another program, called a *loader*, to perform this task. A loader takes a set of machine language instructions as input and loads them into the appropriate memory locations in the hardware. When the loader is finished, the machine language program is ready to run. Obviously, the loader cannot load itself into memory, so this is one of those programs that must be hardwired into the computer.

Now that a loader exists, you can load and run other programs that make the development, running, and management of programs easier. This type of software is called *system software*. The most important example of system software is a computer's *operating system*. You are probably already familiar with at least one of the most popular operating systems, whether Linux, Apple's Mac OS, or Microsoft Windows. Handheld devices use their own versions of operating systems, such as iOS and Android. An operating system is responsible for managing and scheduling several concurrently running programs. It also manages the computer's memory, including the external storage, and manages communications between the CPU, the input/output devices, and other computers on a network. An important part of any operating system is its *file system*, which allows people to organize their data and programs in permanent storage. Another important function of an operating system is to provide *user interfaces*—that is, ways for you to interact with the computer's software. A terminal-based interface accepts inputs from a keyboard and displays text output on a monitor screen. A modern *graphical user interface* (GUI) organizes the monitor screen around the metaphor of a desktop, with windows containing icons for folders, files, and applications. This type of user interface also allows the user to manipulate images with a pointing device such as a mouse or your fingers.

Another major type of software is called *applications software*, or simply applications (or apps on handheld devices). An application is a program that is designed for a specific task, such as editing a document or displaying a web page. Applications include web browsers, word processors, spreadsheets, database managers, graphic design packages, music production systems, and games, among many others.

As you have learned, computer hardware can run only instructions that are written in binary form—that is, in machine language. Writing a machine language program, however, would be an extremely tedious, error-prone task. To ease the process of writing computer programs, computer scientists have developed high-level programming languages for expressing programs. These languages resemble English and allow authors to express their programs in a form that they and other people can understand.

As you have been doing thus far in this book, you start by writing high-level language statements in a text editor. You then run another program called a *compiler* to convert the high-level program code into runnable code. (When you press the F5 key in Python, that's what happens.) Because it is possible for you to make grammatical mistakes even when writing high-level code, the compiler checks for syntax errors before it completes the translation process. If it detects any of these errors, the compiler alerts you via error messages.

If the translation process succeeds without a syntax error, the program can be executed by the runtime system. The runtime system might execute the program directly on the hardware or run yet another program called an *interpreter* or *virtual machine* to execute the program. Figure 4.5 shows the steps and software used in this process for a Python program.

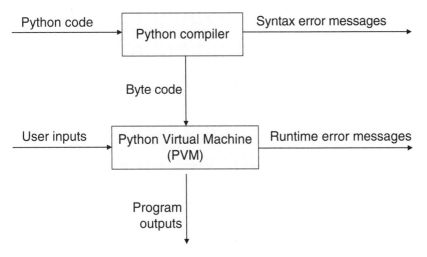

Figure 4.5
Software used to compile and run a program.

If a Python program is well formed, the compiler translates it to an equivalent form in a low-level language called *byte code.*

This byte code is sent to another software component, called the *Python Virtual Machine* (PVM), where it is run. It is here that the PVM further translates the byte code to the machine code of your particular type of computer. If another error occurs during this step, execution halts with an error message.

This concludes your introduction to composing and running Python programs. In the next chapter, you explore some ways to design programs that solve more interesting and complex problems.

SUMMARY

- A program is a sequence of statements that solves a problem.

- The five stages of software development are analysis, design, coding, compilation, and testing.

- In analysis, a programmer states what the various parts of a program will do.

- In design, a programmer states how the parts of a program will solve their assigned tasks.

- In coding, a programmer translates a design into a program in a particular programming language.

- A compiler is a software tool that checks a program for syntax errors and then translates it to a form that a computer can run.

- In testing, a programmer determines whether a program does what it is supposed to do.

- Computer hardware consists of memory, a central processing unit (CPU), and a set of input/output devices.

- The data and instructions of a program are ultimately represented by a set of hardware switches, which can be set to on or off. These physical states in turn can represent the binary digits 1 and 0, which in turn are capable of representing any data or instructions at the machine level.

- Computer memory is a set of switches that store data and programs in machine code (a language of 1s and 0s).

- The central processing unit contains circuitry to carry out basic operations on data in machine code. All computer operations are composed of these basic operations.

- Secondary memory, such as disks and flash sticks, provides permanent storage for data.

- The operating system provides user interfaces for the various input and output devices, such as monitors, keyboards, pointing devices, scanners, cameras, and printers.

- The Python compiler translates Python programs to byte code programs, which are then run on the Python Virtual Machine (PVM).

- System software includes the operating system, text editors (such as IDLE), the Python compiler, and the Python Virtual Machine.

- Application software performs specific tasks, such as word processing and spreadsheet management.

- To run a byte code program, the Python Virtual Machine calls operations in machine language.

EXERCISES

Launch the IDLE shell, open a file window, and complete the following exercises. You should run each program within IDLE and, when it is completed, in the terminal window.

1. Write a Python program, in the file stopsign.py, that draws a stop sign. The sign should be a filled red hexagon with the word "Stop" centered in white letters.

2. Modify the code in samplepattern.py so that it can accept three optional command-line arguments. They represent the number of sides, the outline color, and the fill color, respectively. The program should be able to use one, two, or all three of these arguments. The defaults are as before. Be sure to test your program by running it in a terminal window.

CHAPTER 5

DEFINING FUNCTIONS

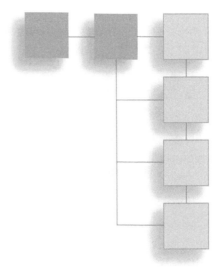

Thus far in this book, your Python programs have consisted of built-in operators, control statements, calls to built-in functions, and one programmer-defined function, main, introduced in the previous chapter.

Strictly speaking, programmer-defined functions are not necessary. You can construct any program using only Python's built-in operators, functions, and control statements. However, in any significant program, the resulting code would be extremely complex, difficult to verify, and almost impossible to maintain.

The problem is that the human brain can wrap itself around just a few things at once. (Psychologists say three things comfortably, and at most seven.) People cope with complexity by developing a mechanism to simplify or hide it. This mechanism is called *abstraction*. Put most plainly, abstraction hides detail and thus allows a person to view many things as just one thing. You use abstractions to refer to the most common tasks in everyday life. For example, consider the expression "doing my laundry." This expression is simple, but it refers to a multistep process that involves fetching dirty clothes from the hamper, separating them into whites and colors, loading them into the washer, transferring them to the dryer, and folding them and putting them into the dresser or closet. Indeed, without abstractions, most of your everyday activities would be impossible to discuss, plan, or carry out. Likewise, effective designers must invent useful abstractions to control complexity.

Design is important in many fields. The architect who designs a building, the engineer who designs a bridge or a new automobile, and the politician, advertising executive, or military commander who designs the next campaign must organize a team and coordinate its members to achieve its objectives. Design is equally important in constructing computer programs, some of which are the most complex artifacts that human beings have ever built. In this chapter, you explore the use of functions to design computer programs.

BASIC ELEMENTS OF FUNCTION DEFINITIONS

In this section, you learn the basic elements of function definitions. These elements include arguments, docstrings, the `return` statement, and optional/keyword/default arguments.

Circles and Squares

Consider what you need to do to draw several circles and squares in a turtle graphics program. To draw a circle, you just move the turtle to the desired position and call the built-in `circle` function with the radius as an argument. But to draw a square of a given length, you have to write the following loop:

```
for count in range(4):
    forward(length)
    left(90)
```

You could copy and paste this code to each place in your program where you want to draw a square, but what if you want to use a different variable or a number for the length? Then you'd still have to edit this code after you copied it. You'd probably agree that calling a function, such as `square`, with the length as an argument, would be a lot easier. For example, the code fragments in the next shell session would draw a circle within a square:

```
>>> reset()
>>> hideturtle()
>>> circle(40)
>>> backward(40)
>>> square(80)
```

Fortunately, as you first saw in Chapter 4, "Composing, Saving, and Running Programs," Python allows you to define your own functions. You can define a `square` function by placing the loop below an appropriate heading, as follows:

```
def square(length):
    """Draws a square with the given length."""
    for count in range(4):
        forward(length)
        left(90)
```

Now you can call the function `square`, just like you call the function `circle`. All you have to do is move the turtle to the desired position and heading and then call the function with an appropriate argument. For example, here is how you would draw a pattern discussed in Chapter 3, "Control Structures: Sequencing, Iteration, and Selection," with the `square` function:

```
for count in range(10):
    square(70)
    left(36)
```

You can define similar functions to draw other geometric shapes, such as hexagons and octagons, as you will see in the exercises.

The simplest form of a Python function definition is

```
def functionName(arguments):
    statements
```

where *arguments* is a series of names separated by commas. Note that each statement in *statements* must be indented below the function's heading.

Docstrings

In Chapter 4, you saw how a *docstring*, the quoted text at the top of a program or module file, describes the purpose of that program or module. As you define new functions to solve problems, you should also document them with docstrings. As shown in your definition of the `square` function, the docstring appears on a line between the function heading and the body of the function. Note that you must indent this string to the same column as the statements within the function. When used in a function definition, a docstring should state what the function does, describe the roles of any arguments, and describe the value, if there is one, that the function returns.

As mentioned in Chapter 4, docstrings allow Python to provide help to the programmer from the shell. When you import a function's module, you can get help on the function by entering `help(moduleName.functionName)` at a shell prompt.

Always write the doctring *before* you write the function's code. This practice helps you clarify what the function does and what roles its arguments play. It also gives the callers of your function, who might be other programmers, valuable information about the use of a resource that you are providing.

The return Statement

The square function defined earlier just draws a square but does not return a value to its caller. The main function discussed in Chapter 4 returns a string value, which is not very interesting. Many other functions, such as Python's math.sqrt function, expect one or more arguments and compute and return a value.

To see how a function can return a value, consider the creation of a random color. In the code examples so far, you have seen that a random color is a tuple containing three random integers, each of which is in the range from 0 to 255. You might create a random color in Python with this code:

```
randomColor = (randint(0, 255), randint(0, 255), randint(0, 255))
```

Here you assign a color value of the appropriate form to the variable randomColor. However, each time you need a new random color, you have to run the same assignment statement (or a different one, if the variable's name changes).

It would be much more convenient if you could call a function named randomColor and then use its value wherever you wanted. You would not have to rewrite or copy and paste a line of complex code every time you wanted a random color. Here is the definition of this function:

```
def randomColor():
    """Returns a random RGB color."""
    return (randint(0, 255), randint(0, 255), randint(0, 255))
```

Note that this function expects no arguments and returns a value. The return statement here includes the Python expression that creates the color value. The next code fragment shows how you might use the function randomColor to draw colored squares in the example pattern:

```
for count in range(10):
    pencolor(randomColor())
    square(70)
    left(36)
```

Here's the form of the return statement:

```
return optionalExpression
```

You can use a return statement to quit a function at any point, even within a loop and even though the function does not return a value. When you omit the expression from a return statement or omit the return statement entirely from a function's statements, that function automatically returns the Python value None.

Testing Functions in a Program

Now that you've seen how to define and call your own functions, you need to know where to put them in Python code files. One way is to write a short tester program. You compose this program in an Integrated DeveLopment Environment (IDLE) file window, just as in Chapter 4. The structure of a tester program now includes the definitions of your functions. Although these definitions can appear in any order in the file, it's common to place them between the `import` section and the `main` function. The next code segment shows a program that tests the functions you have defined thus far in this chapter.

```
"""
testsquare.py
Tester program for square and randomColor functions.
"""

from turtle import *
from random import randint

def square(length):
    """Draws a square with the given length."""
    for count in range(4):
        forward(length)
        left(90)

def randomColor():
    """Returns a random RGB color."""
    return (randint(0, 255), randint(0, 255), randint(0, 255))

def main():
    """Draws a radial pattern with 10 randomly colored squares."""
    speed(0)
    pensize(2)
    colormode(255)
    hideturtle()
    for count in range(10):
        pencolor(randomColor())
        square(70)
        left(36)
    return "Done!"

if __name__ == "__main__":
    msg = main()
    print(msg)
    mainloop()
```

Run this program in an IDLE file window (F5 key). Then import the module `testsquare` in the shell. At that point, you can ask for help on any of the functions, or on the entire module, by running the `help` function with the function or the module name as an argument. You can also run the function `testsquare.randomColor`. Do that a couple of times to view the results. As you experiment with this program, you are also encouraged to add and test new functions, such as a function that draws a hexagon.

Remember to write the docstrings first!

Optional, Default, and Keyword Arguments

Suppose that you want to accept an optional color argument in your `square` function. This argument, if present, allows the caller to draw a square in a new pen color. If this argument is absent, the function draws the square in the current pen color. If the function draws the square in a new color, it restores the old color before returning.

The next code fragment draws a radial pattern of squares using random colors.

```
for count in range(10):
    square(70, randomColor())
    left(36)
```

To define a function with an optional argument, you place the argument name and the default value in what looks like an assignment statement, as shown in the next definition:

```
def square(length, newColor = None):
    """Draws a square with the given length and optional color."""
    if newColor:
        oldColor = pencolor()       # Save old pen color and use new color
        pencolor(newColor)
    for count in range(4):
        forward(length)
        left(90)
    if newColor:
        pencolor(oldColor)          # Restore old pen color
```

Note that the first argument, named `length`, has no default value. This argument is not optional but is required, meaning that the function's caller must supply the length.

If the caller does not supply a second argument when the function is called, the value of `newColor` is automatically `None`. Because Python views this value as `False` and any color value as `True`, you can check for the presence of a new color in a one-way `if` statement.

If the new color is present, you can save the current pen color in the temporary variable oldColor and reset the pen to the new color. Otherwise, if no color argument is present, you can leave the pen color as it is.

After the square is drawn, you check for the presence of the new color once more and restore the old color if the new color exists.

Here are some example calls of this function:

```
>>> square(70)
>>> square(70, "red")
>>> square(length = 70, newColor = "red")
>>> square(newColor = "red", length = 70)
```

The first two calls of the function show just the values of the arguments. The next two calls show the names of the arguments as well as their values. When used in this way, they are called *keyword arguments*. The use of keyword arguments allows you to supply the arguments to a function in a different order than the one shown earlier in the function's definition. However, if you omit the keyword with an argument, that argument must appear in the same position as it was in the function's definition.

FUNCTIONS AS GENERAL SOLUTIONS TO PROBLEMS

Once you become comfortable with defining your own functions, you will start to write them for almost every occasion. But after you've written the code for several functions, you might start to see a common or redundant pattern in them. You might try to find a way to capture this redundancy in a new function, thus saving yourself the trouble of rewriting or copying and pasting the same code. In this section, you examine two ways to do this.

Regular Polygons

The functions square and hexagon are already solutions to general problems, in so far as they allow you to draw a square or a hexagon of any length. However, when you examine the code of each function, you see that the only differences are in the number of sides and the size of the interior angle. Here they are:

```
def square(length):
    """Draws a square with the given length."""
    for count in range(4):
        forward(length)
        left(90)
```

```
def hexagon(length):
    """Draws a hexagon with the given length."""
    for count in range(6):
        forward(length)
        left(60)
```

Both squares and hexagons are examples of a more general type of geometric shape called a *regular polygon*. In a regular polygon, all the sides are the same length and all the interior angles are the same size. Because the interior angle always equals 360 divided by the number of sides, the only variations in these shapes are in fact the length of a side and the number of sides.

Now, can you see a way of defining a new, more general function that allows the caller to draw a regular polygon? Of course, you can; this function, named regularPolygon, takes two arguments: the length and the number of sides. Its loop iterates over the number of sides after computing the appropriate interior angle to use, as follows:

```
def regularPolygon(length, numSides):
    """Draws a regular polygon with the given length
    and number of sides."""
    interiorAngle = 360 / numSides
    for count in range(numSides):
        forward(length)
        left(interiorAngle)
```

Here are some example calls of this function, to draw a square and a hexagon:

```
>>> regularPolygon(70, 4)      # Draw a square of length 70
>>> regularPolygon(70, 6)      # Draw a hexagon of length 70
```

You can also simplify the definitions of the functions square and hexagon, as follows:

```
def square(length):
    """Draws a square with the given length."""
    regularPolygon(length, 4)

def hexagon(length):
    """Draws a hexagon with the given length."""
    regularPolygon(length, 6)
```

If you need to add code to draw a new type of regular polygon, such as a triangle or a pentagon, you can define a specific function like you did for squares and hexagons.

Functions as Arguments

Consider the code that draws a radial pattern of 10 squares:

```
for count in range(10):
    square(70)
    left(36)
```

As you saw in Chapter 4, you can use code such as this to draw a pattern that uses triangles, hexagons, or other regular polygons. At this point, you should be asking yourself this: what must change in this pattern of code to use a different type of polygon in the drawing? Obviously, it's just the name of the function, which in this particular instance happens to be square. If you substitute the name hexagon, the code calls the function to draw hexagons instead.

Unfortunately, you must rewrite the same loop each time you want to draw the pattern. You would like to capture this common pattern of code in a single function. The only thing that would vary from call to call of this function would be the name of the function used to draw the particular type of polygon. If you could pass this function as an argument to a pattern-drawing function, you'd be all set.

Assume that your new pattern-drawing function is named radialPattern. You could call it to draw a square-based pattern and a hexagon-based pattern in the following manner:

```
radialPattern(square)
radialPattern(hexagon)
```

Fortunately, Python is one of the few programming languages that allow you to do this. Here is the code for the definition of the radialPattern function:

```
def radialPattern(polygonFunction):
    """Draws a series of polygons by rotating around a center point."""
    for count in range(10):
        polygonFunction(70)
        left(36)
```

Note that the argument name, polygonFunction in this definition, refers to the function that the caller passes. This function can be square, hexagon, or any function of one argument that draws a polygon.

By now, you should be thinking to yourself, "Hey, this radialPattern function is still not general enough. It always draws a pattern with 10 polygons of length 70. I want to provide a function that can draw *any* number of polygons of *any* length." You'd be right to think that, and in the exercises, you'll have an opportunity to act on that thought.

Building Functions with lambda Expressions

After you get over the shock of learning that you can pass functions as arguments to other functions, you need to learn another related idea.

You saw earlier that you can define any function to draw a particular type of regular polygon by calling the more general function `regularPolygon`. The arguments to this function are the length of a side and the number of sides. When you want to draw a new type of polygon, you just define a function for it in this manner and call that function.

However, there are lots of regular polygons besides the standard ones with three, four, five, six, and eight sides. Defining a new function for each one can get rather tedious, when you could simply call the `regularPolygon` function to perform the desired task. But you can't pass this function as an argument to the `radialPattern` function. That's because `regularPolygon` expects two arguments, whereas `radialPattern`'s function argument expects only one argument—the length of a side—when it is called.

Fortunately, Python provides a nice way around this problem. When you defined the `square` function, you essentially "wrapped" a call of `regularPolygon` with two arguments inside of a function, `square`, that expects one argument. Python includes a special form called a `lambda` expression that allows you to do just that, without going to the trouble of defining a named function. The form of a Python `lambda` expression follows:

`lambda arguments: expression`

Suppose, for example, that you want to draw a 16-sided figure. The following `lambda` expression builds a new function that would do the trick:

```
>>> lambda length: regularPolygon(length, 16)
<function <lambda> at 0x102b69ef0>
```

This `lambda` expression is evaluated in a shell session to show you that a function is built and returned. This is an *anonymous function* of one argument, the length, which is just what you need for `radialPattern`. When your new function is eventually called, it calls `regularPolygon` to draw a regular polygon with 16 sides. Here is a sample call of your new function, which draws a 16-sided polygon of length 70:

```
>>> (lambda length: regularPolygon(length, 16))(70)
```

Pass this `lambda` expression as an argument to the `radialPattern` function to draw the pattern with a 16-sided polygon:

```
>>> radialPattern(lambda length: regularPolygon(length, 16))
```

To change the particular type of polygon, you only have to change the number of sides.

MODULES AS LIBRARIES OF FUNCTIONS

By now you will have written several related functions for drawing geometric shapes and perhaps a few patterns that use these shapes. You should continue to test your functions in short tester programs. But as the number of functions grows, you need a better place to keep them, where you can access them just like you access Python's library functions `math.sqrt` and `random.randint`.

After you test each function and verify that it's working as expected, you should place it in an appropriate module or library file. Call your first module `mygeometry`. You create this file by opening a new file window in IDLE. Immediately save this file with the name `mygeometry.py`. Then add a doctring at the top of the file that summarizes the purpose of this module. At that point, you can start to paste in each function definition as it becomes available.

Every so often, you should import your new module into one of the tester programs you've used and run your functions as module functions. If you use the form

```
moduleName.functionName(argumentList)
```

when calling your functions, you can be sure that they will be available for any programmers who eventually use your module.

MATH TOPIC: GRAPHING FUNCTIONS

In this section, you learn how you can use functions in a Python program to express functions as understood in mathematics.

Functions in Mathematics

There are several ways to express a function in mathematics. In algebra, a function f expresses a relationship between two variables, x and y. In shorthand, this relationship is stated as the equation

$$y = f(x)$$

In this equation, f is the function, y is the *dependent variable*, and x is the *independent variable*. This means that, for the function f, as you change the value of x, the value of y also changes. The set of all values that x can take on is called the function's *domain*, and the set of all values that y can take on is called the function's *range*.

A function f expresses a rule for mapping the values of its domain into the corresponding values in its range. For example, take the function that expresses the square of a given number x, also known as x^2. Subsets of this function's domain and range are shown in Table 5.1.

Table 5.1   A Subset of the Domain and Range of $y = x^2$

x (Domain)	y (Range)
1	1
2	4
3	9
4	16

In each row of this table, you can see that the value of y is the square of the value of x.

To state the rule for a function f, you must expand this function into an expression that uses x to compute the corresponding value of y. This expression can consist of operators and applications of other functions to the value of x. For example, you can expand the function $f(x)$ to the expression $x * x$ or $x ** 2$ to state the rule for expressing the square of x. Thus, for this case, the equation $y = f(x)$ expands to the equation $y = x * x$ (or $y = x ** 2$, if you use the exponentiation operator).

Another way to express a function is to draw a graph that plots a given subset of its domain. Each point (x, y) on this plot represents the solution to the equation $y = f(x)$ for a given value of x. The values of x are plotted along the x-axis, and the values of y are plotted along the y-axis. Figure 5.1 shows the graphs of two equations, $y = 2 * x + 10$ and $y = x ** 2 - 10 * x + 3$. The first equation is also called a *linear equation*, and the second equation is also called a *quadratic equation*.

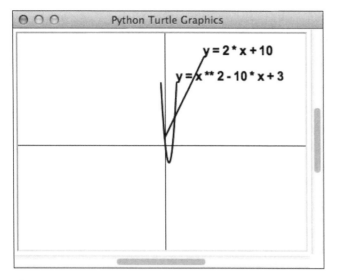

Figure 5.1
Graphs of two functions.
© 2014 Python Software Foundation.

Graphing Functions in Turtle Graphics

You'll develop a simple function that plots a given function, $f(x)$, for a set of values, $x_1 .. x_n$, in the function's domain. Expressing each function $f(x)$ is easy in Python. For example, here are the two functions graphed in Figure 5.1:

```
def quadratic(x):
    """A quadratic function."""
    return x ** 2 - 10 * x + 3

def linear(x):
    """A linear function."""
    return 2 * x + 10
```

The function that plots the graph of another function is called `plot`. The `plot` function accepts another function as an argument. In all, the `plot` function expects four arguments:

- The function to be plotted

- The lower bound of the domain

- The upper bound of the domain

- A string that labels the plotted function

Thus, to plot the two functions as shown in Figure 5.1, you would call the following:

```
plot(linear, 0, 50, "y = 2 * x + 10")
plot(quadratic, -5, 15, "y = x ** 2 - 10 * x + 3")
```

In the `plot` function, you raise the pen and position it at the first point (x, y) generated by applying the argument function. You then lower the pen and loop through the remaining x values in the domain. On each pass through the loop, you apply the function to compute a y value and go to the new (x, y) position. When the loop finishes, the last step writes the label at the final (x, y) position. Here is the code for the `plot` function:

```
def plot(f, x1, x2, label):
    """Plots f(x) for the domain x1..x2."""
    up()
    y = f(x1)
    goto(x1, y)
    down()
    for x in range(x1 + 1, x2 + 1):
        y = f(x)
        goto(x, y)
    write(label, font = ("Arial", 16, "bold"))
```

A helper function draws the axes to the dimensions of the canvas, and the size of the pen is set to 2 before plotting the functions for clarity. The development of the complete program is left as an exercise for you.

REFACTORING A PROGRAM WITH FUNCTIONS

The process of modifying a program to make it simpler to read and maintain is called *refactoring*. In this section, you explore how to refactor the code for a random walk, introduced in Chapter 3. Here is the code for the second version of that program:

```
from turtle import *
from random import randint
reset()
width = window_width()                              # Line 4
height = window_height()
(minX, maxX) = (-(width / 2), width / 2)
(minY, maxY) = (-(height / 2), height / 2)
(x, y) = position()
while x > minX and y > minY and x < maxX and y < maxY:  # Line 9
    distance = randint(10, 60)                      # Line 10
    forward(distance)                               # Line 11
```

```
degrees = randint(45, 135)                 # Line 12
if randint(1, 2) == 1:
    left(degrees)
else:
    right(degrees)                         # Line 16
(x, y) = position()                        # Line 17
```

In this version of the program, the turtle moves a random distance and then turns left or right a random number of degrees until it moves past one of the edges of the window. At that point, the turtle stops and the program ends.

Simplifying the Code for the Random Walk

If you study the code for the random walk closely, you will spot several major tasks that function calls could simplify:

Lines 4–9 and line 17 are run to determine whether the turtle has crossed an edge of the window. This code could be packaged in a Boolean function named atEdge. This function returns True if the turtle's position has crossed an edge, or False otherwise. Moreover, because the window's dimensions are examined each time the function is called, the turtle can continue if the user grows the window or stop sooner if the user shrinks the window.

Lines 11 and 12 move the turtle forward a random distance. This code could go in a function named randomForward, which expects the bounds of the possible distances as arguments.

Lines 12–16 turn the turtle left or right by a random number of degrees. You could place this code in a function named randomTurn, which expects the bounds of the possible degrees as arguments. You could also add a third, optional argument that specifies the probability of making a turn.

Before you define each of these new functions, you should rewrite the code for the top-level program (now in a main function) to see how your functions are used:

```
from turtle import *
from random import randint

# New function definitions will go here

def main():
    reset()
    while not atEdge():
        randomForward(1, 3)        # Move 1, 2, or 3 units
        randomTurn(45, 135, .05)   # Turn 1/20 of the time
```

As you can see, you have just reduced 15 lines of code to 4 lines of code and made the top-level program easier to read and understand. You can also supply arguments that move the turtle shorter distances and turn it fewer times to smooth the pattern of the walk. Now it's time to complete the program by defining the functions.

The atEdge Function

As a first cut at defining the atEdge function, you simply move the code from the earlier program into a new function definition, as follows:

```
def atEdge():
    """Returns True if the turtle is at an edge of the window,
    or False otherwise."""
    width = window_width()
    height = window_height()
    (minX, maxX) = (-(width / 2), width / 2)
    (minY, maxY) = (-(height / 2), height / 2)
    (x, y) = position()
    return x > minX and y > minY and x < maxX and y < maxY
```

Before you move on to the other functions, consider how you might simplify the code of the atEdge function, while adding some other potentially useful functions. The atEdge function determines whether the turtle has crossed an edge. This will be True if the turtle crosses the top edge, the bottom edge, the left edge, or the right edge. By expressing it in this way and imagining that you have four new functions at your disposal, you can rewrite the code for atEdge as follows:

```
def atEdge():
    """Returns True if the turtle is at an edge of the window,
    or False otherwise."""
    return atTopEdge() or atBottomEdge() or \
           atLeftEdge() or atRightEdge()
```

Each of the four new edge-detection functions compares one of the turtle's coordinates to a single boundary coordinate. For instance, here is the code for the topEdge function:

```
def atTopEdge():
    """Returns True if the turtle is at the top edge of the window,
    or False otherwise."""
    return ycor() > window_height() / 2
```

The other three functions have a similar pattern of code. You will use these new functions to create a more realistic random walk shortly.

The randomForward Function

The `randomForward` function might contain the two lines of code that pick a random distance and move the turtle forward by that amount. But you can make this function a bit more flexible than that, as follows:

```
def randomForward(lower, upper = None):
    """Moves the turtle a random distance, from lower through upper.
    If upper is absent, moves turtle the lower distance"""
    if not upper:
        distance = lower
    else:
        distance = randint(lower, upper)
    forward(distance)
```

You might be surprised to see that the second argument, upper, has a default value of None. This, together with the if-else statement, allows the caller to move the turtle forward either a random distance or a given distance. Thus, the randomForward function will work just as expected in the random walk program, but will also be helpful when used in a slightly different way in other programs.

The randomTurn Function

The `randomTurn` function has one required argument and two optional arguments.

As in the `randomDistance` function, the first two arguments are named lower and upper, and they work together in a similar manner. If the value of upper is absent, the turn is not random, and the value of lower is the number of degrees used to take the turn. If they are both present, a random number from lower through upper is chosen to specify the number of degrees.

The third argument is named probability, and it specifies the probability of the turtle's turning. The default value of this argument is 1, meaning that the turn will be made. Any value less than 1 means that the turn might not be taken at all.

As you can imagine, this function requires substantial control logic. Here is the code, followed by an explanation:

```
def randomTurn(lower, upper = None, probability = 1):
    """Turns the turtle a random number of degrees, from
    lower through upper.
    If upper is absent, turns the turtle by the lower amount of degrees.
    Probability represents the likelihood of making the turn."""
    from random import choice
```

```
# Determine whether to make a turn first.
if probability < .01:         # Probability too small to take the turn
    return
if probability < 1:           # Maybe not take the turn
    if not choice(range(100)) in range(0, int(probability * 100)):
        return

# A turn will be made, so the # of degrees is either random or given
if not upper:                 # Upper absent, so use lower
    degrees = lower
else:                         # Choose a random amount of degrees
    degrees = randint(lower, upper)

if randint(1, 2) == 1:        # Turn left or right with equal prob.
    left(degrees)
else:
    right(degrees)
```

Whew! There is a saying that nothing good comes cheaply, and this function is a case in point. Whenever there is complex logic, you try to handle the easiest cases first. So, here are the cases in this function:

1. The probability is less than .01, so you just quit the function.

2. The probability is less than 1, so you use it to determine whether to continue. You pick a random number from 0 through 99 and then see if that number is in the range of numbers from 0 through 100 times the probability. If it's not in that range, you quit the function.

3. If you get this far, you'll be turning the turtle. If the value of upper is not present, the number of degrees will be the value of lower. Otherwise, the number of degrees is a random number from lower through upper.

4. Finally, you choose whether to turn left or right, with equal probability.

Note that the function also imports the random function choice for later use in its code.

Even though you have expended a lot of effort on several new function definitions, this effort will be well rewarded. Your top-level code will be simpler and easier to read and manage. Moreover, other programmers will find your code useful, should you decide to share it with them.

Another Version of the Random Walk

The random walk program halts when the turtle crosses an edge of the window. But animals don't typically stop when they encounter obstacles; they either climb over them or turn to try another route.

Another version of a random walk allows the turtle to turn back into the enclosed area of the window when it encounters an edge. In this version, the main loop runs a definite number of times—perhaps long enough to allow the turtle several "rebounds" off the edges of its window. When the turtle crosses an edge, it turns its back to that edge and proceeds from there. Otherwise, it takes a random turn, as before. The program also allows the user to specify the number of iterations via a command-line argument. This value is 1000 by default.

Here is the code for the new version of the program:

```
from turtle import *
from random import randint
import sys

# New function definitions will go here

def main():
    if len(sys.argv) > 1:
        iterations = int(sys.argv[1])
    else:
        iterations = 1000
    reset()
    for count in range(iterations):
        randomForward(1, 3)            # Move 1, 2, or 3 units
        if atTopEdge():
            setheading(270)            # Go south
        elif atBottomEdge():
            setheading(90)             # Go north
        elif atLeftEdge():
            setheading(0)              # Go east
        elif atRightEdge():
            setheading(180)            # Go west
        else:
            randomTurn(45, 135, .05) # Turn 1/20 of the time by default
```

As you can see, the functions you developed in this section have come in quite handy. You will have many more occasions to structure your code with functions in the rest of this book.

SUMMARY

- A function definition consists of a heading and a set of statements.

- A function heading contains the function's name and a parenthesized list of argument names.

- A function's docstring is located between the function's heading and its statements.

- A default argument appears as an assignment of a default value to the argument's name in a function heading.

- If an argument has a default value, you can omit that argument when the function is called.

- Arguments can be passed with keywords when a function is called. The keyword is the argument's name, which is followed by the assignment operator and its value. A keyword argument may appear in a different position than its position in the function definition's heading.

- An argument without a keyword must appear in the same position in both the call and the definition of the function.

- An argument without a default value must appear before any of the arguments with defaults in the function definition's heading.

- An argument without a default value is required; you cannot omit it when the function is called.

- The `return` statement returns the value of an expression to the function's caller. When the expression is omitted or the function has no `return` statement, that function returns the value `None`.

- A function may be passed as an argument to another function.

- The `lambda` expression creates an anonymous function.

EXERCISES

Launch the IDLE shell, open a file window, and complete the following exercises. You should run each program within IDLE and, when it is completed, in the terminal window.

1. The Pythagorean Theorem defines the relationship between the hypotenuse of a right triangle and its other two sides. It states that the square of the hypotenuse is equal to the sum of the squares of the other two sides. Define a function named `hypo`

that expects the lengths of other two sides of a right triangle as arguments. This function returns the triangle's hypotenuse. Include this function in a tester program that exercises its capabilities.

2. Try to use the regularPolygon function to draw circles. Note what happens when you vary the length. Then define a new function named myCircle, which expects the radius of the circle as an argument. This function should call regularPolygon with the appropriate arguments to draw a circle with the given radius. Include this function in a tester program that exercises its capabilities. Hint: determine the radius of a circle that is a regular polygon with a length of 1 and 360 sides. Then use that information to determine the length to be used for any given radius.

CHAPTER 6

USER INTERACTION WITH THE MOUSE AND THE KEYBOARD

In the previous two chapters, you wrote programs that drew shapes in a turtle graphics window. However, many other programs take information as input from people. This information might be text (like a username and password) or numbers (like your age or income tax paid). Text and numbers are entered from the keyboard. People might also interact with a program by moving a mouse, clicking it, or dragging it. Many programs, especially computer games, would be unthinkable without such input capabilities. In this chapter, you explore various ways of allowing users to interact with your turtle graphics programs.

USING DIALOG-BASED INPUT

In Chapter 4, "Composing, Saving, and Running Programs," you learned how some programs obtain input via command-line arguments. For example, when you run the command

examplepattern.py 6 blue pink

the program draws a radial pattern of hexagons with a blue pen color and a pink fill color. This way of taking input into a program is fine for some applications, but it has two shortcomings:

- Most people don't run programs from a terminal window.
- When they do, it may not be clear to them what role the input plays in the program. In this program, which color is the pen color, and which color is the fill color? And what does the 6 mean?

Most people are used to receiving an informative prompt for a computer input; such a prompt describes the type of value that's requested. In terminal-based Python programs, Python's input function serves this purpose, but again, most people don't run programs from a terminal window. Moreover, even when you do run a turtle graphics program from a terminal, your program code can no longer access the terminal window for input values.

The primary way in which window-based applications receive input is via labeled entry fields within a window. As you know from filling in forms on the web, you place the mouse cursor in a box and type in the number or text requested. The request or prompt is a label that appears next to the field. You then click a Submit or OK button to inform the program that the input is ready, or you click a Cancel button to back out of the input operation altogether. Turtle graphics supports this strategy for input with input dialogs, which form the subject of this section.

Input Dialogs in Turtle Graphics

An *input dialog* is a small window that pops up for input. The window contains a message about the kind of data requested and a field for the user to enter this information via the keyboard. Command buttons are available to submit or cancel the input.

Assume that the pattern drawing program of the previous two chapters takes three inputs from input dialogs. At program start-up, the user is presented with a sequence of three dialogs, shown in Figure 6.1.

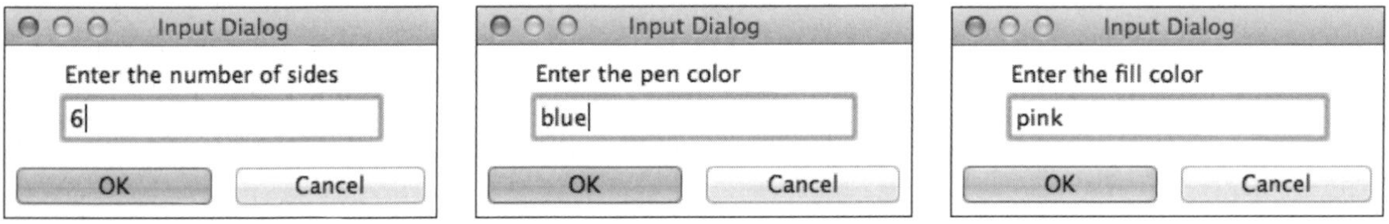

Figure 6.1
Three input dialogs.
© 2014 Python Software Foundation.

When the user closes each dialog, the next one pops up, until all the input has been submitted or canceled. If input is canceled, the program uses a default value, as before.

Turtle graphics dialogs come in two flavors: one for accepting numbers, and the other for accepting strings. The two functions for input dialogs are named textinput and numinput. Now you'll examine these functions more closely.

Input Dialogs for Text

The `textinput` function obtains a string input. The function expects a title and a prompt as arguments. If the user clicks the dialog's OK button, the dialog returns the string contained in the input field. Otherwise, the user has clicked Cancel or has simply closed the dialog window, so the dialog returns the Python value `None`. The program has to check for this value after the `textinput` function returns to make sure that some text has actually been entered.

Here is the code that inputs the pen color in your program after setting the default input values and inputting the number of sides:

```
(numSides, outline, background) = (6, "blue", "yellow")
# Input the number of sides here first (see exercises)
datum = textinput("Input Dialog", "Enter the pen color")
if datum:
    outline = datum
```

Note that if the user clicks OK and the dialog's input field happens to be empty, the `textinput` function returns the empty string. In the context of the `if` statement, the empty string behaves just like the value `False`. Therefore, the `outline` variable in that case retains its default value (set earlier in the program), just as if the user had canceled or simply closed the dialog.

Input Dialogs for Numbers

The `numinput` function obtains a numeric input. The function expects a title and a prompt as arguments. Optional arguments include a default input number, a minimum acceptable number, and a maximum acceptable number. When the dialog pops up, the default number is displayed in the input field if that number is supplied as an argument; otherwise, the field is empty. If the minimum or maximum argument is supplied, the dialog checks the user's input number against these limits before returning. If the number is out of this range, the dialog displays a message and waits for more input. Like the text input dialog, a numeric dialog returns `None` if the user cancels or closes the window; otherwise, it returns the input as a floating-point number.

Here is the code that inputs the number of sides in the example program:

```
datum = numinput("Input Dialog",
                 "Enter the number of sides [3-8]",
                 default = 6, minval = 3, maxval = 8)
if datum:
    numSides = int(datum)
```

The nice thing about using the `minval` and `maxval` arguments is that they free you from checking the input value later with your own code. But note that this program must later convert the input value to an `int` because `numinput` returns it as a `float`.

The complete sequence of input operations in this program is left as an exercise for you.

RESPONDING TO MOUSE EVENTS

Perhaps you have used a paint program, which allows you to make drawings by dragging the mouse around on a virtual sketchpad. To do this in turtle graphics, you have to be able to detect mouse events and respond to them. The turtle graphics system recognizes the three types of mouse events listed in Table 6.1.

Table 6.1   Mouse Events

Mouse Event	When It Happens	Example
Click	The user presses and releases the mouse button, without moving the mouse.	The user selects a file icon.
Drag	The user presses the mouse button and moves the mouse while continuing to press the button.	The user drags a file icon from one window to another.
Release	The user releases the mouse button.	The user releases the mouse button when the icon of a file is over the trashcan icon.

In this section, you explore how to detect and respond to mouse events in turtle graphics.

Drawing Line Segments with Mouse Clicks

To enable turtle graphics to respond to a mouse event, you need to perform two steps:

1. Let turtle graphics know which function it should call when a given type of mouse event, such as a click, occurs. This function is called an *event-handling function*.

2. Tell turtle graphics to start listening for events.

Suppose you want turtle graphics to call its `goto` function whenever the user clicks the mouse anywhere in the turtle graphics window. To do this, you pass the `goto` function as an argument to the function `onscreenclick` (Step 1). You then call the `listen` function, which instructs turtle graphics to listen for events in its window (Step 2). When you click the mouse in that window, the turtle moves from its current position to the mouse click position.

These operations are so simple that you can experiment with them in the shell. For example, the following shell session allows you to draw line segments by clicking the mouse. A sample drawing is shown in Figure 6.2.

```
>>> from turtle import *
>>> shape("circle")
>>> pencolor("blue")
>>> width(2)
>>> onscreenclick(goto)
>>> listen()
```

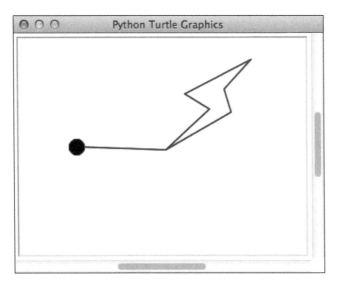

Figure 6.2
Drawing with mouse clicks.
© 2014 Python Software Foundation.

Note that you should call the `listen` function only after all the event-handling functions have been set, although in this case, there is only one of these.

Turtle graphics includes another function, `onclick`, which registers a function to handle mouse clicks that occur within the boundaries of the turtle's shape. You should experiment with the use of `onclick` in a session similar to the one just shown.

How Event Handling Works

Even after you have told turtle graphics which function should handle a given mouse event and told it to start listening for events, nothing happens until an event occurs. In the example you just saw, turtle graphics is ready to call the goto function whenever you click the mouse in its window. When you do that, turtle graphics passes the current mouse coordinates as arguments to the goto function, and the turtle moves to that new position. So event handling is automatic once you have told turtle graphics which functions to use and readied it to listen for events. The only thing you have to do, in the case of a mouse event, is to provide an event-handling function that expects two arguments. These arguments represent the (x, y) coordinates of the current mouse position.

Freehand Drawing by Dragging the Mouse

Drawing line segments with mouse clicks, as you did just now, is pretty simple but also pretty rigid. You can only draw straight lines, and you can't pick the pen up and put it down again without drawing another line segment. A true freehand drawing program allows you to drag the virtual pen around with the mouse and draw curved lines as well as straight ones. When you let go of the mouse button, you can move the virtual pen to a new position without drawing anything.

Turtle graphics allows you to respond to mouse drag events with the ondrag function. Like the onscreenclick function, the ondrag function expects another function as an argument. The latter function is triggered repeatedly, while the user drags the mouse from one position to another in the turtle graphics window. Initially, you must position the mouse on the turtle's shape for the first drag event to be detected. As before, the event-handling function's two arguments will be the current mouse coordinates.

To experiment with ondrag in the shell, you can pass it the goto function, just as you did with onscreenclick earlier. Figure 6.3 shows a sample drawing. Here is the new shell session:

```
>>> from turtle import *
>>> shape("circle")
>>> pencolor("blue")
>>> width(2)
>>> ondrag(goto)
>>> listen()
```

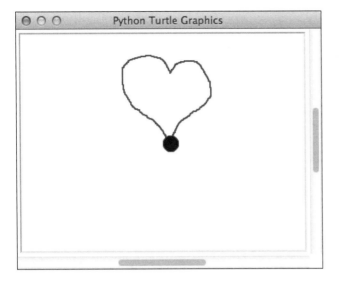

Figure 6.3
Drawing by dragging the mouse.
© 2014 Python Software Foundation.

This technique works well for drawing line segments that are connected, but it fails when you want to pick up the pen to move to a new position (say, to draw the smiley face shown in Figure 6.4). To move to a new position without drawing, your code needs to respond to a mouse click event as well. But this time, instead of simply calling `goto`, which draws a line segment to the new position, you must pick up the pen, call `goto`, and put the pen back down when a click event occurs. You can package these steps in a function named `skip` and then pass that function to `onscreenclick` to handle the click events.

Here is a complete Python program that provides these two capabilities:

```
"""
sketching1.py
Simple drawing by dragging the mouse; also allows movement by clicking.
"""

from turtle import *

def skip(x, y):
    """Moves the pen to the given location without drawing."""
    up()
    goto(x, y)
    down()

def main():
    shape("circle")
```

```
    width(2)
    speed(0)
    pencolor("blue")
    ondrag(goto)                    # Register the two event-handling functions
    onscreenclick(skip)
    listen()
    return "Done!"
if __name__ == "__main__":
    msg = main()
    print(msg)
    mainloop()
```

Figure 6.4
Dragging to draw and clicking to move.
© 2014 Python Software Foundation.

RESPONDING TO KEYBOARD EVENTS

Believe it or not, early computer systems did not include a mouse. In these systems, all the commands to do things had to come from the keyboard. In modern computer systems, you can still use some keyboard combinations, such as Ctrl+s or Command+s, to save a file. Furthermore, you can use the arrow keys to move up, down, left, or right through the text in a window.

Some early computer systems allowed people to use the keyboard to sketch drawings. For example, you might use the right and left arrow keys to draw forward and backward, the "l" and "r" keys to turn left and right, the "u" and "d" keys to pick the pen up and put it down, and the "c" key to clear the drawing window. In this section, you learn how to respond to keyboard events in the same manner as you responded to mouse events earlier in this chapter.

The onkey Function

Turtle graphics can recognize two keyboard events: a key press and a key release. There are two functions to register event handlers for these events: onkeypress and onkeyrelease. In this section, you learn about the function onkey, which is a synonym for onkeyrelease.

The function onkey expects two arguments: a function and a keyboard value. The keyboard value is either a string containing the single character on a given keyboard key or a string reserved for a special key, such as an arrow key. The onkey function binds a given key to a given function, meaning that when the key is released, the function is called. For example, if you issue the command onkey(down, "d"), Python binds the "d" key to the down function, and the pen is placed down when the user releases the "d" key. As before, you set up all your event handlers for the different keys and then call the listen function to start listening for events.

To experiment with key events, you can bind the arrow keys to move the turtle forward or backward, turn it left or right, and clear the drawing, as shown in the following shell session:

```
>>> from turtle import *
>>> pencolor("blue")
>>> speed(0)
>>> width(2)
>>> onkey(clear, "c")
>>> onkey(lambda: forward(5), "Right")
>>> onkey(lambda: back(5), "Left")
>>> onkey(lambda: right(5), "r")
>>> onkey(lambda: left(5), "l")
>>> listen()
```

Note several points about this code:

- "Right" identifies the right arrow key, whereas "r" identifies the key containing that letter.

- The movement and rotation functions use a distance of 5 units and an angle of 5 degrees, respectively, for faster interaction.

- All but one of the event-handing functions are provided as lambda expressions. You first saw lambda expressions in Chapter 5, "Defining Functions." You use a lambda expression here to create a no-argument function that calls a function of one argument. Key events can only trigger no-argument functions, so the `lambda` expression here does the trick.

A Complete Retro Drawing Program

You can now marshal your knowledge of keyboard events to write a complete Python program to make drawings with the keyboard. Here is the code:

```
"""
sketching2.py
Simple drawing with the keyboard.
All movements and turns are by increments of 5.
Right arrow key = move forward
Left arrow key = move backward
r = turn right
l = turn left
u = pen up
d = pen down
h = go home
c = clear
"""

from turtle import *

def main():
    width(2)
    speed(0)
    pencolor("blue")
    onkey(up, "u")
    onkey(down, "d")
    onkey(clear, "c")
    onkey(home, "h")
    onkey(lambda: forward(5), "Right")
    onkey(lambda: back(5), "Left")
    onkey(lambda: left(5), "l")
    onkey(lambda: right(5), "r")
    listen()
    return "Done!"

if __name__ == "__main__":
    msg = main()
    print(msg)
    mainloop()
```

USING MODULE VARIABLES

In the programs you have written thus far, you have used variables to track various kinds of information, such as a pen color input by the user or the coordinates of a point that are the arguments in a function definition. When you manipulated these variables, either to use their values or to reset them, you usually did so within the body of a function definition. For example, you used variables to receive inputs in the main function or to access arguments in the skip function. Variables of this sort are considered to be *local* to that function, meaning that their values are accessible only within the body of that function and not outside of it (either in another function or in the surrounding module).

Local variables may be of no help when you need to track information that several functions should know about. For example, the functions that respond to mouse events know the turtle's current position, but not its previous one. In this section, you examine the use of another kind of variable, called a *module variable*, which allows you to share this information among different functions.

Initializing and Using Module Variables

You have seen several module variables in your turtle graphics programs thus far—the variables __main__ and msg in the if statement at the end of each program. The variables math.pi and sys.argv are also module variables, although they belong to another module that your program module imports. The math module assigns the variable pi its value. Python automatically assigns __main__ and sys.argv their values when a program is run. Your program assigns msg its value. Each name is a module variable because it is assigned a value outside the bodies of any function definitions.

After a module variable has been assigned a value, you can access this value anywhere within the module, including within the bodies of function definitions. The next short Python program demonstrates the introduction and use of another module variable for π:

```
"""
modulevariables.py
"""

PI = 3.14              # Module variable (instead of math.pi)
def area(radius):
    return PI * radius ** 2
def volume(radius):
    return 4 / 3 + PI * radius ** 3
def main():
    radius = 4.5
    print("PI:", PI)
```

```
    print("Radius:", radius)
    print("Area:", area(radius))
    print("Volume:", volume(radius))
if __name__ == '__main__':
    main()
```

Note that the variable PI is assigned a value above any of the function definitions. Thus, it is a module variable, and its value is accessible everywhere in the module. Because PI behaves like a constant in this program, you set its value just once. The only restriction on the use of a module variable is that you cannot assign it a new value within a function definition. You will see how to get around that limitation shortly.

Tracking the History of Turtle Positions

Now, suppose you need to know the positions that the turtle has recently visited. For example, you might write a program that allows the user to draw a triangle with three mouse clicks. Each click will be on a vertex of the triangle, and the turtle will connect them with line segments to complete the drawing. The first line-drawing program won't be able to do this. (Try it yourself; you'll need four clicks.)

To draw a triangle with just three clicks, your program needs a different strategy. On the first mouse click, the turtle skips to that position, without drawing. On the second mouse click, the turtle draws a line segment connecting the first two vertices. On the third mouse click, the turtle draws two more line segments to complete the figure.

To support this capability, you need to record the positions of earlier clicks somewhere, and you need to make some choices based on the number of clicks that have already occurred. A list would work fine for that; it would start out empty, and you could append each position to the list when the mouse is clicked. Here are the rules for making choices, based on the length of this list:

- If the list is empty, skip to the click position and add the click position to the list.

- If the list contains one position, go to the click position (drawing a line segment from the first position) and add the click position to the list.

- If the list contains two positions, draw line segments from each of them to the click position, and make the list empty again.

All this code goes in the event-handling function for mouse clicks. Name that function setVertex. As usual, the function expects two arguments: the coordinates of the mouse click. The function assumes that the variable positionHistory refers to a list of the positions of the most recent mouse clicks. Now the only remaining question is this: where is this variable initialized to the empty list?

Because the variable `positionHistory` must retain its value between function calls, it must be a module variable. Thus, it is initialized near the beginning of the module, just like you did with `PI` in the earlier example. Here is the code for the complete program:

```python
"""
triangle.py

Draws triangles with 3 mouse clicks.
"""

from turtle import *

positionHistory = []

def setVertex(x, y):
    """Sets vertices and possibly connects them."""
    if len(positionHistory) == 0:               # The first click skips
        positionHistory.append((x, y))          # to the first vertex
        skip(x, y)
    elif len(positionHistory) == 1:             # The second click connects
        positionHistory.append((x, y))          # two vertices
        goto(x, y)
    else:
        (xCoord, yCoord) = positionHistory.pop()  # The third click
        skip(xCoord, yCoord)                      # connects the remaining
        goto(x, y)                                # vertices
        (xCoord, yCoord) = positionHistory.pop()
        goto(xCoord, yCoord)

def skip(x, y):
    "Moves the pen to the given location without drawing."
    up()
    goto(x, y)
    down()

def main():
    shape("circle")
    width(2)
    speed(0)
    pencolor("blue")
    onscreenclick(setVertex)
    listen()
    return "Done!"
```

```
if __name__ == '__main__':
    msg = main()
    print(msg)
    mainloop()
```

Because the third click empties the position history list, you can continue to draw new triangles at other positions.

USING TWO MOUSE BUTTONS

As you probably know, a mouse usually has at least two buttons, located on the left and the right of the top surface of the device. Clicking the left button is called a left-click, and clicking the right button is called a right-click. For mice that do not have a right button, you can perform a right-click by holding the Ctrl key while clicking the left button.

You probably accomplish most of your mouse-related tasks by clicking or holding down the left button, but the right button occasionally comes in handy. For example, a right-click often pops up a menu of options related to the context of your current window. In this section, you learn how to respond to a right-click in turtle graphics, to add some command options to your applications.

Adding an Event-Handling Function for the Right Button

Each type of mouse event in turtle graphics—a click, a drag, or a release—can result from a press of the left button or the right button. The functions onscreenclick, onclick, ondrag, and onrelease allow you to specify separate event-handling functions for the left and the right buttons. You do that by supplying a second optional argument to these functions. Table 6.2 lists their headings.

Table 6.2   Functions That Register Event-Handling Functions for Mouse Events

Function	What It Does
onscreenclick(fun, btn=1, add=None)	Registers fun to handle a click event anywhere in the window.
onclick(fun, btn=1, add=None)	Registers fun to handle a click event on the turtle.
ondrag(fun, btn=1, add=None)	Registers fun to handle a drag event on the turtle.
onrelease(fun, btn=1, add=None)	Registers fun to handle a release event on the turtle.

As you can see, the event-handling function `fun` is a required argument, and the button number `btn` is an optional argument. (Remember: arguments that have no = following them are required.) The default button number is 1, signifying the left mouse button. That's the option you have used for any mouse events so far in this chapter. But if you supply 2 as a second argument, turtle graphics binds the right mouse button to your event-handling function for that event. Thus, your function is triggered when the user manipulates the right mouse button.

The `add` option by default replaces any existing event-handling functions for the specified button with the new function. But if you supply the value `True` for this argument, turtle graphics adds your new function to the set of functions to be triggered when that event occurs. Thus, you can register multiple event-handling functions for both buttons for all four of the mouse events.

Example 1: Simple Drawing with Random Colors

To experiment with the use of right mouse button, you can return to sketching in the shell. In this session, you register the `goto` function for screen clicks with the left mouse button. This draws a line segment between the turtle's position and the position of the left-click. (See Figure 6.2 earlier in this chapter.) You also register a `lambda` expression for screen clicks with the right mouse button. This expression builds a function that sets the pen color to a random color. Here is a transcript of this session:

```
>>> from turtle import *
>>> from random import choice
>>> colors = ("red", "blue", "green", "purple", "orange")
>>> shape("circle")
>>> onscreenclick(goto)
>>> onscreenclick(lambda x, y: pencolor(choice(colors)), btn = 2)
>>> listen()
```

Now when you left-click, the turtle draws a line segment, as before. But when you right-click, the turtle's pen color resets to a randomly chosen color (which may be the same color as the previous one, because the set of colors here is pretty small).

Example 2: Drawing and Moving

Now instead of changing the pen color, suppose you want to move the turtle to a new position without drawing a line segment. You can do this with a right-click by binding the right button to the `skip` function discussed earlier in this chapter. Here is how you could do that in a shell session:

```
>>> from turtle import *
>>> def skip(x, y): up(); goto(x, y); down()

>>> shape("circle")
>>> onscreenclick(goto)
>>> onscreenclick(skip, btn = 2)
>>> listen()
```

Note the use of the semicolons in the definition of the `skip` function. They allow you to write separate Python statements on a single line of code, for a more concise presentation.

Example 3: Drawing, Moving, and Random Colors

Suppose you want a right-click to both move the turtle to a new position and change its color. To do this, you register both event-handling functions with the right-click, being careful to supply an optional `add` argument of `True` when you register the second function. Here is the code for this version:

```
>>> from turtle import *
>>> from random import choice
>>> colors = ("red", "blue", "green", "purple", "orange")
>>> def skip(x, y): up(); goto(x, y); down()

>>> shape("circle")
>>> onscreenclick(goto)
>>> onscreenclick(lambda x, y: pencolor(choice(colors)), btn = 2)
>>> onscreenclick(skip, btn = 2, add = True)
>>> listen()
```

The two event-handling functions associated with the right button fire in the order in which they were registered by `onscreenclick`.

Example 4: Dialogs for Shape Properties

Perhaps you would like to draw some polygons interactively at different positions in the turtle graphics window. Each polygon has a length, a number of sides, and a color. Given these properties, you can position a polygon anywhere in the window with a left-click of the mouse. A right-click should allow you to change any of the attributes of the next polygon to be drawn. A series of pop-up dialogs allows you to enter this information (length, number of sides, and color). As a first cut, here is a program that allows you to draw a polygon with default properties:

```
"""
drawpolygon1.py
Draw polygons with a left-click.
"""

from turtle import *

properties = {"length":30, "numSides":4, "color":"black"}

def regularPolygon(length, numSides):
    """Draws a regular polygon.
    Arguments: the length and number of sides."""
    interiorAngle = 360 / numSides
    for count in range(numSides):
        forward(length)
        left(interiorAngle)

def skip(x, y):
    "Moves the pen to the given location without drawing."
    up()
    goto(x, y)
    down()

def moveAndDraw(x, y):
    """Draws a polygon with the current properties at
    position (x, y)."""
    skip(x, y)
    pencolor(properties["color"])
    regularPolygon(properties["length"], properties["numSides"])

def main():
    width(2)
    speed(0)
    hideturtle()
    onscreenclick(moveAndDraw)
    listen()
    return "Done!"

if __name__ == "__main__":
    msg = main()
    print(msg)
    mainloop()
```

This program sets up the default properties of the polygon in a module variable named properties. This variable is initialized to a dictionary, and each property is stored as a key/value pair there. The dictionary initially contains the default values of all the properties. The dictionary makes it easy for you to access or change any property, as well as add new properties to improve the program.

There are two things you need to do to allow the user to change the properties. First, you define an event-handling function that runs when the user clicks the right mouse button. This function, named changeProperties, expects the coordinates of the mouse click, which are ignored. The function then takes the user through a series of three pop-up dialogs, which allow him to reset the polygon's length, number of sides, and color. Here is the code for this new function:

```python
def changeProperties(x, y):
    """Obtains new values for the polygon's properties from
    the user and resets them in the properties dictionary."""
    length = numinput("Input Dialog", "Enter the length",
                      default = properties["length"], minval = 1)
    if length:
        properties["length"] = int(length)
    numSides = numinput("Input Dialog", "Enter the number of sides",
                        default = properties["numSides"], minval = 3)
    if numSides:
        properties["numSides"] = int(numSides)
    color = textinput("Input Dialog", "Enter the color")
    if color:
        properties["color"] = color
```

The second change is to register the changeProperties function as the event handler for the right button, with the onscreenclick function. You do this in the main function, as follows:

```python
def main():
    width(2)
    speed(0)
    hideturtle()
    onscreenclick(moveAndDraw)
    onscreenclick(changeProperties, btn = 2)
    listen()
    return "Done!"
```

You can easily extend this design to include properties for the fill color and pen size. You add defaults for these properties to the dictionary and the appropriate input dialogs to the changeProperties function. The rest is automatic.

This concludes your introduction to user interaction with turtle graphics. You can now write some programs that really engage people.

SUMMARY

- The user can provide interactive inputs to a turtle graphics program by means of pop-up dialogs. Turtle graphics provides two types of dialogs: one for numbers and one for text.

- The textinput function is used to pop up a dialog for a string (a single line of text). The function expects the dialog's title and a prompt as string arguments. If the user cancels or closes the dialog, the function returns None. Otherwise, if the user clicks OK, the function returns the string contained in the input field.

- The numinput function is used to pop up a dialog for an input number. The function expects the dialog's title and a prompt as string arguments. Optional arguments include a default numeric value, a minimum allowable value, and a maximum allowable value. If the user cancels or closes the dialog, the function returns None. Otherwise, if the user clicks OK, the function checks the text in the input field for correct format, converts this text to a number, and checks it against any optional bounds. If an error occurs, the dialog informs the user and waits for more input. Otherwise, the number is returned as a float.

- The user can also interact with a turtle graphics program if that program is set up to respond to mouse events and keyboard events.

- The four mouse events in turtle graphics are a click in the window, a click on the turtle's shape, a drag on the turtle's shape, and a release on the turtle's shape.

- The programmer responds to a mouse event by providing an event-handling function. This function is triggered when an event of that type occurs.

- The functions to register event-handling functions for mouse events are onscreenclick, onclick, ondrag, and onrelease. Each of these functions expects an event-handling function as an argument. When triggered, this function is passed the coordinates where the mouse event occurred.

- Optional arguments to onscreenclick, onclick, ondrag, and onrelease are the number of the button (1 = left, 2 = right) and a Boolean value indicating whether to add the new event-handling function or replace the existing ones.

- The functions to register event-handling functions for keyboard events are onkeypress and onkeyrelease (a synonym for onkey). onkeypress expects a function and an optional string as arguments. onkeyrelease expects both a function and a string as arguments. The string represents a keyboard character. When the user presses or releases a registered key, the associated event-handling function is triggered. If the string argument to onkeypress is omitted, the function is triggered when any key is pressed.

- After the event-handing functions have been registered, the listen function tells turtle graphics to listen for events.

- A module variable is used to make data accessible to all the functions in a module. A module variable cannot be reset with an assignment statement within a function. However, if the variable refers to a mutable structure, like a list, that structure can be modified.

EXERCISES

Launch the IDLE shell, open a file window, and complete the following exercises. You should run each program within IDLE and, when it is completed, in the terminal window.

1. Write a pattern-drawing program similar to the one discussed in Chapters 4 and 5. This version uses dialogs to take the length of a side, the number of sides, the pen color, and the fill color as inputs via dialogs.

2. Write a program that allows the user to draw circles with two mouse clicks. The position of the first click will be the circle's center point, and the position of the second click will be a point on the circle's circumference. Hint: the function distance(x, y) returns the distance from the turtle's current position to the position (x, y). Also, use a module variable to remember the position of the first mouse click.

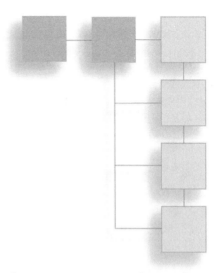

CHAPTER 7

RECURSION

Computer science is sometimes called the science of abstraction. As you learned in Chapter 5, "Defining Functions," an abstraction is a means of simplifying a complex situation or problem. For example, the term *word processing* refers to all the things you might do with text, including editing text, checking the spelling and grammar of text, and saving text to files, among other things. Each of these apparently simple processes, in turn, is an abstraction of other processes.

In this chapter, you learn an especially beautiful and elegant way to create abstractions called *recursion*. A recursive situation or problem can be subdivided into smaller situations or problems of the same form. Along the way, you learn how to construct recursive functions to solve such problems and explore some recursive patterns in art and nature.

RECURSIVE DESIGN

Recursive design is a variation of an important design strategy called top-down design. In this section, you review the top-down design of a program from Chapter 5, as a prelude to learning about the important features of recursive design.

Top-Down Design

One popular design strategy for programs of any significant size and complexity is called *top-down design*. This strategy starts with a global view of the entire problem and breaks the problem into smaller, more manageable subproblems—a process known as *problem decomposition*. As each subproblem is isolated, its solution is assigned to a function.

Problem decomposition may continue down to lower levels, because a subproblem might in turn contain two or more lower-level problems to solve. As functions are developed to solve each subproblem, the solution to the overall problem is gradually filled out in detail. This process is also called *stepwise refinement*.

For example, consider the problem of plotting the graph of a function, for which you wrote a program in Chapter 5. The solution to this problem required you to perform several subtasks:

■ Initialize the turtle's state.

■ Draw the axes.

■ Compute the value of y for each value x in a set of values in a function's domain.

■ Draw line segments between the resulting (x, y) points in the graph.

You assigned each of these tasks to a Python function and coordinated their actions within a top-level main function. The relationships among the programmer-defined functions are depicted in the *call diagram* of Figure 7.1.

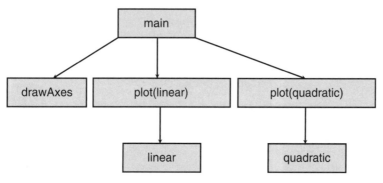

Figure 7.1
The call diagram of the function-plotting program.

Note that program execution begins with the main function at the top of the diagram. This function calls the functions shown in the next level below, from left to right. The functions not shown, such as speed, are built in. Others, like plot, are defined by you and call still other functions at a lower level to do their work.

There are four important points to note about top-down design:

■ You typically begin with a main function, which simply calls other functions to accomplish its task. This part of design is easy, because you simply think of appropriate names and arguments for these functions and let them worry about how they do their jobs. In other words, passing the buck and procrastination are virtues!

- You continue to pass the buck at each level of the design. To complete each function, you think of other functions to call, with the appropriate arguments.

- The buck appears to stop when you call a built-in function.

- Although there is occasionally some overlap, the subtasks in a top-down design are typically different from each other and thus call for different functions to perform them.

Recursive design shares some of these characteristics with top-down design but also differs in important ways, as you will see in the next subsection.

Recursive Function Design

In recursive design, a problem is broken into subproblems of the same form. In these cases, you assign each subproblem to the same function as the one that solves the problem at a higher level. A function of this sort is called a *recursive function*.

For example, consider the problem of computing the summation of a sequence of integers from a lower bound to an upper bound. The function summation(1, 4) should return the result of 1 + 2 + 3 + 4, or 10. One way to design a solution to this problem is to recognize that this sequence of additions contains the following nested summations:

```
summation(1, 4) = 1 + summation(2, 4)
summation(2, 4) = 2 + summation(3, 4)
summation(3, 4) = 3 + summation(4, 4)
summation(4, 4) = 4
```

Note that the last case, summation(4, 4), is not composed of another summation but simply returns one if its arguments. Figure 7.2 shows a call diagram for summation(1, 4).

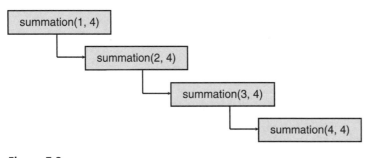

Figure 7.2
A call diagram of summation(1, 4).

Note that each call of the summation function, with the exception of the last one, calls summation again. This call is known as a *recursive call* of the function.

The final call of the summation function makes no recursive call but instead returns one of the arguments directly. This is known as the *base case* of the function.

On each recursive call of the function, the first argument increases by 1. As this value increases, it eventually reaches a limit that stops the recursive process. In other words, this adjustment allows the function to detect when the recursion should stop and return the base case value.

Now, can you come up with a general formula for the summation function from its recursive description? Of course you can. You assume that the summation function has two arguments, named low and high. As their names imply, you also assume that low is less than or equal to high whenever the function is called. So the recursive formula for the summation function is expressed as two equations. The first equation expresses what a summation is when the two arguments are equal (the final call in Figure 7.2). The second equation expresses what a summation is otherwise. Here are the two equations:

```
summation(low, high) = high, if low == high
summation(low, high) = low + summation(low + 1, high)
```

You should review Figure 7.2 to verify that these two equations describe the partial summations contained in summation(1, 4) before continuing.

You can turn this design into an implementation by defining a Python function named summation. This function states the assumptions about the arguments in a docstring and then uses a two-way if statement to express the two options stated in the design. Here is the code for the function, embedded in a short tester program:

```
"""
File: recursion1.py
Define and test a recursive summation function.
"""

import sys
def summation(low, high):
    """Returns the summation of the integers
    from low to high.
    Precondition: low <= high."""
    if low == high:
        return high
    else:
        return low + summation(low + 1, high)
```

```
def main(low = 1, high = 4):
    if len(sys.argv) == 3:
        low = int(sys.argv[1])
        high = int(sys.argv[2])
    print("The summation of", low, "and", high,
            "is", summation(low, high))
if __name__ == "__main__":
    main()
```

Note that the main function here includes default arguments of 1 and 4, which are passed on to the summation function when the program launches. You can then test the function by calling main in the shell with other arguments, as shown in the next session:

```
>>>
The summation of 1 and 4 is 10
>>> main(1, 10)
The summation of 1 and 10 is 55
>>> main(2, 10)
The summation of 2 and 10 is 54
>>>
```

Because the program also checks for command-line arguments, you can test the program in a terminal window as well:

```
Madison:~ ken$ python3 recursion1.py
The summation of 1 and 4 is 10
Madison:~ ken$ python3 recursion1.py 1 10
The summation of 1 and 10 is 55
```

Recursive Function Call Tracing

To get a better understanding of how a recursive function works, it is helpful to trace its calls. You'll do that for the summation function. You add an argument for a margin of indentation and print statements to trace the two arguments and the value returned on each call. The first statement on each call computes the indentation, which is then used in printing the two arguments. The value computed is also printed with this indentation just before each call returns. Here is the code for the summation function with tracing:

```
def summation(low, high, margin = 0):
    """Returns the summation of the integers
    from low to high. Prints a trace of low,
    high, and the value returned for each call,
```

```
    using the given margin.
    Precondition: low <= high."""
    blanks = " " * margin
    print(blanks, low, high)
    if low == high:
        print(blanks, high)
        return high
    else:
        result = low + summation(low + 1, high, margin + 4)
        print(blanks, result)
        return result
```

Note that the expression " " * margin builds a string that contains the number of blank spaces specified by the margin operand. This value is initially 0 when the function is called and increases by 4 on each recursive call. Thus, each pair of arguments is indented further to the right as the recursion proceeds down to the base case. When control returns to each caller, the previous value of margin is restored, so the return values are undented further to the left as the recursion unwinds. Here is sample trace of summation(1, 4):

```
>>>
 1 4
     2 4
         3 4
             4 4
             4
         7
     9
 10
The summation of 1 and 4 is 10
>>>
```

As you can see from this trace, the value of the first argument increases on each recursive call until it equals the value of the second argument. As the recursive calls return, the value of the summation increases.

Recursive Functions and Loops

By now, you may have guessed that a recursive function repeats a given process until a condition becomes False. If you think that sounds like a loop, you're right. In principle, you can rewrite any recursive function as a loop, and you can rewrite any loop as a recursive function. The choice between recursion and iteration is partly a matter of programmer taste and partly a matter of performance requirements.

The recursive summation function developed in this section might seem elegant and graceful to the eye, but each call at runtime requires an extra chunk of computer memory to support the storage for the arguments and return values. Thus, the amount of memory required to run this function grows as a linear function of the size of the range of numbers being summed. For small ranges, this is not a significant problem, but for large ranges, a loop-based summation provides a better alternative.

The loop-based version of the summation function uses a for loop with the range function and adds each value to an ongoing total. The total is initially set to 0 and is returned when the loop finishes. Here is the code:

```
def summation(low, high):
    """Returns the summation of the integers
    from low to high.
    Precondition: low <= high."""
    total = 0
    for number in range(low, high + 1):
        total += number
    return total
```

Why is the runtime performance of this version better than the recursive version? The loop-based function is called just once, with memory allocated for the two arguments low and high and for the temporary variables total and number. On each pass through the loop, the values in this storage are reset, but no new storage is ever added or ever needed.

So now you might ask, "Why do I need to bother with recursion at all, if a loop-based function seems to perform better than a recursive one?" There are two cases in which you might still prefer a recursive alternative.

The first reason you might prefer recursion is that it allows you to write some recursive functions that do not result in growth of memory usage at runtime. These functions are called *tail-recursive functions*. In a tail-recursive function, no operation is performed after a recursive call. The recursive summation function defined earlier is not, on this definition, tail recursive. After each recursive call of summation returns, its total is added to the previous value of the low argument, in the following statement:

```
return low + summation(low + 1, high)
```

To convert such a function to a tail-recursive function, you need to think of a way of passing the total as an extra argument to each function call. Then you can increase the total at runtime *before* each recursive call, rather than after. In the case of the summation function, the total is initially 0, and it is returned directly when `low` becomes greater than `high`. When `low` is less than or equal to `high`, `summation` is called recursively, as follows:

```
summation(low + 1, high, low + total)
```

The `total` argument has a default value of 0, so it doesn't need to be provided on the top-level call of the `summation` function. Here is the complete code for the tail-recursive version:

```
def summation(low, high, total = 0):
    """Returns the summation of the integers
    from low to high.
    Precondition: low <= high."""
    if low > high:
        return total
    else:
        return summation(low + 1, high, low + total)
```

Although this function looks like it might be called multiple times, a smart compiler can translate the Python code to a loop-based version that uses a fixed amount of memory for the three arguments and the single value returned if `low` is greater than `high`. Thus, it becomes a matter of your Python taste whether you use this version or the loop-based version of the function, because they are both loop based at runtime.

The second reason you might prefer recursion is that some loop-based solutions also require a linear growth of computer memory at runtime. In those solutions, your code manipulates a Python data structure called a *stack*, which schedules other data values for processing by the loop. As the size of the problem grows, so does the stack. In this case, a recursive solution performs no less efficiently than an iterative solution but might be preferred on the grounds of taste or simplicity. You will see examples of such problems later in this chapter.

Infinite Recursion

As you design and use recursive functions, you need to be aware of a potential error that can occur in their use. Like loops, recursive functions have to have a way of stopping and returning with a solution to a problem. Thus, you have to be careful to move the process along so that you can reach the base case.

For example, the first version of the summation function increments the value of the first argument until it equals the value of the second argument:

```
def summation(low, high):
    """Returns the summation of the integers
```

```
    from low to high.
    Precondition: low <= high."""
    if low == high:
        return high
    else:
        return low + summation(low + 1, high)
```

This code works correctly as long as `low <= high` on the top-level call. (Note the precondition in the docstring.) But suppose you run the program in the terminal window, with `low` initially greater than `high`, as follows:

```
Madison:~ ken$ python3 recursion1.py 2 1
Traceback (most recent call last):
  File "recursion1.py", line 25, in <module>
    main()
  File "recursion1.py", line 22, in main
    "is", summation(low, high))
RuntimeError: maximum recursion depth exceeded in comparison
Madison:~ ken$
```

The program halts with a runtime error message, called an *infinite recursion*. Because the first argument is greater than the second one and continues to be incremented, it never has a chance to equal the second argument. Thus, the recursive calls cannot stop. The only reason they don't continue forever is that the Python virtual machine (PVM) runs out of memory to support additional calls of the function. That is, when the number of recursive calls reaches a maximum depth, the PVM raises an exception, and the program crashes.

The key to avoiding such errors is to warn the users of your function about the preconditions on its arguments. Remember to include that information in docstrings!

Sequential Search of a List

Before you explore the use of recursion in turtle graphics, you'll explore the design of a recursive function for searching a list. Python has two operations for searching a list. The first operator, the `in` operator, returns `True` if an item is in the list, or `False` otherwise. The second operator, the `index` method, returns the position of the item if it's in the list or raises an exception otherwise. The following session shows their use:

```
>>> fruits = ["apples", "bananas", "grapes", "oranges"]
>>> fruits
['apples', 'bananas', 'grapes', 'oranges']
```

```
>>> "grapes" in fruits
True
>>> "cherries" in fruits
False
>>> fruits.index("grapes")
2
>>> fruits.index("cherries")
Traceback (most recent call last):
  File "<pyshell#5>", line 1, in <module>
    fruits.index("cherries")
ValueError: 'cherries' is not in list
>>>
```

Both operations perform a *sequential search*. This means that the search starts with the first item in the list, compares it to the target item, and continues from there through consecutive positions until the target is located or the end of the list is reached.

Writing your own sequential search function for the in operation can help you understand this process. There are two base cases in this function. Either you have reached the end of the list or the item at the current position equals the target item. You return False in the first case and True in the second case. Otherwise, you apply the search function recursively to the rest of the list after the current position. This recursive strategy is formalized in the following pseudocode:

```
Function myIn(targetItem, lyst, currentPosition = 0)
    If currentPosition == len(lyst)
        Return False
    Else if lyst[currentPosition] == targetItem
        Return True
    Else
        Return myIn(targetItem, lyst, currentPosition + 1)
```

Your design translates quite easily to the corresponding Python code:

```python
def myIn(targetItem, lyst, currentPosition = 0):
    if currentPosition == len(lyst):
        return False
    elif lyst[currentPosition] == targetItem:
        return True
    else:
        return myIn(targetItem, lyst, currentPosition + 1)
```

Binary Search of a List

Your sequential search function works as advertised, but it does not run as quickly as it could with the given list. A sequential search like this one has a *linear running time*, meaning that the amount of time it takes to run the search grows directly with the length of the list. For example, in the worst case, you must examine each item to determine that the target item "cherries" is not in the list. If the list contains 100 items, 100 recursive calls are required, and if the list grows in length by a factor of 10, so does the number of recursive calls.

Why should a search perform better than that with this particular list? If you look closely, you see that the items in the list are strings in ascending order. If the items are guaranteed to be in sorted order, your search function can take advantage of this fact to reduce the search time considerably.

The strategy for this type of search, called a *binary search*, is simple. You go to the midpoint of the list, instead of the first item, and compare the item at that position to the target item. If the two items are equal, you're done. Otherwise, if the target item is less than the item at the midpoint, you continue the search in the part of the list to the left of the midpoint. Otherwise, the target must be greater than the item at the midpoint, so you search only the part of the list to the right of the midpoint.

Instead of always searching the rest of the list to the right of the current position, as in sequential search, the binary search examines *either* the segment of the list to the right *or* the segment of the list to the left of the current position. Because the binary search function is recursive, you have to feed it arguments that tell it the leftmost and rightmost positions of the current list segment under examination.

The only things left to determine are how to compute the midpoint, how to adjust the endpoints before the recursive calls, and how to determine when there are no more items left to examine. If you assume that left and right are the current endpoints of the list, the midpoint between them is always

```
(left + right) // 2
```

If the target item is less than the item at the midpoint, the new right endpoint becomes

```
right = midpoint - 1
```

If the target item is greater than the item at the midpoint, the new left endpoint becomes

```
left = midpoint + 1
```

As the search moves around in the list, the two endpoints left and right eventually converge toward a crossover point somewhere within the list. When they move past each other, there are no more items to examine, and the target item is not present. So, as long as

```
left <= right
```

the search must continue.

Your new version of the myIn function keeps its header and defines a recursive helper function named binaryIn. This function takes the left and right endpoints of the list as arguments. Their initial values are 0 and the length of the list minus one, respectively. Here is the complete code for the new version of myIn:

```
def myIn(targetItem, lyst):
    def binaryIn(left, right):
        if left <= right:
            midpoint = (left + right) // 2
            if lyst[midPoint] == targetItem:
                return True
            elif targetItem < lyst[midPoint]:
                return binaryIn(left, midpoint - 1)
            else:
                return binaryIn(midPoint + 1, right)
        else:
            return False
    return binaryIn(0, len(lyst) - 1)
```

Recall that the sequential search function must examine every item in the worst case, when the target item is not present. Thus, in this case, if there are 16 items, the sequential search function must make 16 recursive calls. Just how much faster is the binary search function? The binary search discards half of the remaining list items before each recursive call. So, how many recursive calls must be made before you discover that a target item is not in a list? That number is equal to the number of times that you can divide the length of the list by 2 before you reach a list segment whose length is 0. For example, for a list of length 16, the recursive calls examine list segments of lengths 8, 4, 2, 1, and 0. That's a maximum of 5 calls, whereas the sequential search requires a maximum of 16 calls. Put mathematically, the binary search has a *logarithmic running time* (5 equals $1 + \log_2$ of 16, where the $\log_2$ of a number is the exponent used with 2 to obtain that number). This means that the running time grows only logarithmically with the size of the list. That is, when the size of the list doubles, the amount of work that the binary search performs does not double, but increases by just 1 recursive call!

RECURSIVE PATTERNS IN ART: ABSTRACT PAINTING

The twentieth century Dutch artist Piet Mondrian developed a style of abstract painting that exhibited simple recursive patterns. To generate such a pattern with a computer, you begin with a rectangle drawn in a random color and then repeatedly draw two unequal subdivisions with random colors. Several sample drawings are shown in Figure 7.3 (actual colors not shown).

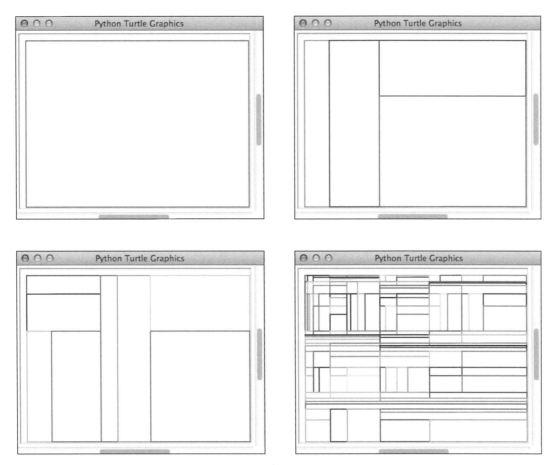

Figure 7.3
Generating simple recursive patterns in the style of Piet Mondrian.
© 2014 Python Software Foundation.

As you can see, the program continues the process of subdivision until an "aesthetically right moment" is reached. In this version, the program divides the current rectangle into portions representing one-third and two-thirds of its area and randomly alternates these subdivisions along the horizontal and vertical axes. The user of the program specifies the level of detail in the drawing. In Figure 7.3, you see, from left to right, a level-1 drawing, a level-3 drawing, a level-4 drawing, and a level-8 drawing.

In this section, you develop the parts of a program to create drawings like the ones in Figure 7.3. The exercises give you an opportunity to add embellishments.

Design of the Program

Your art-drawing program appears in a single module file named mondrian.py. As usual, the program consists of a main function and several supporting functions. Because you are drawing in random colors, you can use the randomColor function discussed in Chapter 5. Also, because you might be drawing many rectangles, you will define a drawRectangle function. Finally, you will define a function to draw a complete artwork. This function's name is, appropriately, mondrian. Figure 7.4 shows the call diagram for the programmer-defined functions.

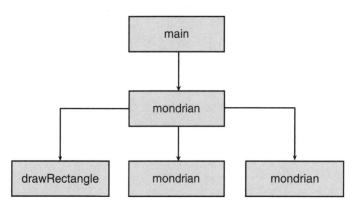

Figure 7.4
The call diagram for the mondrian program.

As you can see, the main function makes a single call to the mondrian function. This function then makes a call to the drawRectangle function and calls itself (recursively) twice. You will learn in a moment how to stop these recursive calls.

Performance Tracking

Just for fun, you can maintain some statistics on the performance of the program. These data include the number of rectangles drawn and the number of calls of the mondrian function. You keep these values in a dictionary named stats, which is set up as a module variable. This variable is initialized near the beginning of the module, and its data are reset to 0 at the beginning of the main function. Here is the code to initialize stats:

```
# Data to track performance
stats = {"calls":0, "rectangles":0}
```

You increment the number of calls each time that mondrian is called, and you increment the number of rectangles each time that drawRectangle is called. You will use these statistics to analyze the program's behavior shortly.

The drawRectangle Function

Unlike the functions you developed for drawing geometric shapes in Chapter 5, the drawRectangle function expects the coordinates of two corner points—the upper-left corner and the lower-right corner—as arguments. In this case, you can draw the rectangle's line segments by calling the goto function. Before these line segments are drawn, you must obtain a random color, set the pen to that color, pick up the pen to move a corner point, and place the pen down. The remaining steps, which draw the four line segments with goto, require you to figure out the correct coordinates for the other two corner points. Here is the code for the drawRectangle function:

```
def drawRectangle(x1, y1, x2, y2):
    """Draws a rectangle with the given corner points
    using a random color."""
    stats["rectangles"] = stats["rectangles"] + 1
    (red, green, blue) = randomColor()
    pencolor(red, green, blue)
    up()
    goto(x1, y1)
    down()
    goto(x2, y1)
    goto(x2, y2)
    goto(x1, y2)
    goto(x1, y1)
```

The mondrian Function

The mondrian function expects the coordinates of two corner points of a rectangle and a level number as arguments. The function draws a complete artwork for that level. Now, what does that last sentence really mean?

Suppose the function receives a level of 3 on its top-level call. A level-3 drawing consists of two rectangles, each of which is a level-2 drawing. Each of these, in turn, consists of two rectangles, each of which is a level-1 drawing. A level-1 drawing is a simple rectangle containing no smaller rectangles.

The main point here is that you use the same mondrian function to create all these drawings, as long as their levels are greater than or equal to 1. Each one is drawn on either the top-level call or a recursive call of mondrian.

When does the recursion stop? When the level becomes 0. In that case, the function simply returns and does nothing. Here is a pseudocode design for this recursive process:

```
Function mondrian(x1, y1, x2, y2, level)
    If level > 0
        Call drawRectangle(x1, y1, x2, y2)
        Compute the corner points of two smaller rectangles
        Call mondrian with one set of corner points and level - 1
        Call mondrian with the other set of corner points and level - 1
```

As you can see, because the level decreases by 1 on each recursive call, it will eventually reach 0, and the recursion will stop.

The most complicated part of the mondrian function is the computation of the corner points of the two new rectangles. There are many options here. The simplest strategy would be to locate the corner points of the two rectangles given by a vertical line through the middle of the current rectangle. However, if you do this every time, you'll see a boring series of evenly spaced vertical lines in the drawing.

A better alternative is to subdivide the current rectangle either vertically or horizontally, with equal probability. In addition, you can split the current rectangle into unequal areas, perhaps using fractions of 1/3 and 2/3 of the current rectangle's size.

The following Python code for the mondrian function uses this strategy. You will have an opportunity to refine it in the exercises.

```python
def mondrian(x1, y1, x2, y2, level):
    """Draws a Mondrian-like painting at the given level."""
    stats["calls"] = stats["calls"] + 1
    if level > 0:
        drawRectangle(x1, y1, x2, y2)
        vertical = randint(1, 2)
        if vertical == 1:  # Vertical split
            mondrian(x1, y1, (x2 - x1) / 3 + x1, y2,
                     level - 1)
```

```
        mondrian((x2 - x1) / 3 + x1, y1, x2, y2,
                level - 1)
    else:                    # Horizontal split
        mondrian(x1, y1, x2, y1 - (y1 - y2) / 3,
                level - 1)
        mondrian(x1, y1 - (y1 - y2) / 3, x2, y2,
                level - 1)
```

The main Function

You conclude with the code for the main function. This function performs the following steps:

1. Prompt the user for the level of the drawing. Level 1 will be the default and the minimum value allowed.

2. Initialize the turtle. The turtle will be hidden, its pen size will be 2, and its speed will be 0.

3. Compute the coordinates of the upper-left and lower-right corners of the initial rectangle. To show the outermost within the current boundaries of the turtle graphics window, provide a margin of 20 pixels.

4. Call the mondrian function with the rectangle's coordinates and the level as arguments.

Here is the code for the main function:

```
def main():
    # Reset the stats on each call of main.
    stats["calls"] = 0
    stats["rectangles"] = 0
    # Obtain the level from the user.
    level = numinput("Input Dialog", "Enter the level",
                    default = 1, minval = 1)
    if not level:
        level = 1
    paintingWidth = window_width() // 2 - 20    # Offset within edge of
    paintingHeight = window_height() // 2 - 20 # window.
    hideturtle()
    speed(0)
    pensize(2)
```

```
# Delay drawing if level is greater than 6.
if level > 6:
    tracer(False)
mondrian(-paintingWidth, paintingHeight,
        paintingWidth, -paintingHeight, level)
# Draw now if level is greater than 6.
if level > 6:
    update()
```

The tracer and update Functions

Note that you call the tracer function before calling the mondrian function, if the level is greater than 6. When called with an argument of False, the tracer function delays any drawing until the update function is called. The update function is called in the matching if statement after the mondrian function finishes. In between, the turtle still does all the computations for the drawing in the mondrian function, but no output occurs until update is called. If you did not do this for large levels, it would take a long time to draw all the rectangles in the figure.

Generally, input and output operations are much slower than other computations, which occur at the speed of light within the CPU. But despite this move to speed up the output, even the internal computations are not fast enough to prevent considerable delays, as the size of the level grows quite large.

Just how large is this rate of growth in the mondrian function? Table 7.1 shows the number of calls of the mondrian function and the number of rectangles drawn for levels 1 through 5.

Table 7.1 Performance Statistics of the mondrian Function

Level	Number of Rectangles	Number of Calls
1	1	3
2	3	7
3	7	15
4	15	31
5	31	63
N	2^N-1	$2^{N+1}-1$

As you can see, the amount of work (and ultimately, the running time) of the `mondrian` function increases more quickly than the square of the size of the level. In each case, there are exactly 2^N-1 rectangles drawn, where N is the level. For very large levels (say, greater than 20), the program eventually completes its task, but not in a reasonable amount of time. (Run the expression `2 ** 20-1` in the shell to see how many rectangles would be drawn for a level-20 figure.)

Note that this *exponential rate of growth* is the inverse of the logarithmic rate for the binary search function that you saw earlier in this chapter. Unfortunately, there is no way to improve on the exponential behavior of the `mondrian` function. Fine art can be expensive!

RECURSIVE PATTERNS IN NATURE: FRACTALS

Fractals are highly repetitive or recursive patterns. A fractal object appears geometric, yet it cannot be described with ordinary Euclidean geometry. Strangely, a fractal curve is not one dimensional, and a fractal surface is not two dimensional. Instead, every fractal shape has its own fractal dimension. To understand what this means, you start by considering the nature of an ordinary curve, which has a precise finite length between any two points. By contrast, a fractal curve has an indefinite length between any two points. The apparent length of a fractal curve depends on the level of detail in which it is viewed. As you zoom in on a segment of a fractal curve, you can see more and more details, and its length appears greater and greater. Consider a coastline, for example. Seen from a distance, it has many wiggles but a discernible length. Now put a piece of the coastline under magnification. It has many similar wiggles, and the discernible length increases. Self-similarity under magnification is the defining characteristic of fractals; it's seen in the shapes of mountains, the branching patterns of tree limbs, and many other natural objects.

One example of a fractal curve is the *c-curve*. Figure 7.5 shows the first six levels of c-curves and a level-10 c-curve.

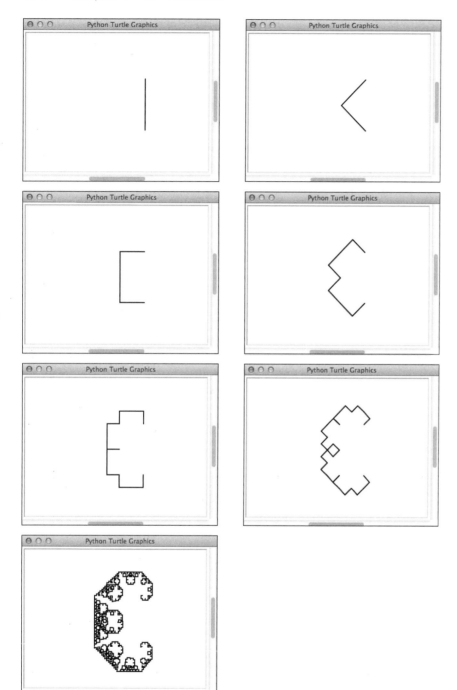

Figure 7.5
C-curves of levels 0 through 6 and a c-curve of level 10.

The level-0 c-curve is a simple line segment. The level-1 c-curve replaces the level-0 c-curve with two smaller level-0 c-curves that meet at right angles. The level-2 c-curve does the same thing for each of the two line segments in the level-1 c-curve. This pattern of subdivision can continue indefinitely, producing quite intricate shapes. In the remainder of this section, you develop a function that uses turtle graphics to display a c-curve.

What the Program Does

The program prompts the user for the level of the c-curve. After this integer is entered, the program displays a turtle graphics window in which it draws the c-curve.

Design of the Program

You can draw an N-level c-curve with a recursive function. The function receives the endpoints of a line segment and the current level as arguments. At level 0, the function draws a simple line segment. Otherwise, a level N c-curve consists of two level $N-1$ c-curves, constructed as follows:

```
Let xm be (x1 + x2 + y1 - y2) // 2
Let ym be (x2 + y1 + y2 - x1) // 2
```

The first level $N-1$ c-curve uses the line segment (x1, y1), (xm, ym) and level $N-1$, so the function is called recursively with these arguments.

The second level $N-1$ c-curve uses the line segment (xm, ym), (x2, y2) and level $N-1$, so the function is called recursively with these arguments.

For example, in a level-0 c-curve, let (x1, y1) be (50, -50) and (x2, y2) be (50, 50). Then, to obtain a level-1 c-curve, use the formulas for computing xm and ym to obtain (xm, ym), which is (0, 0). Figure 7.6 shows a solid line segment for the level-0 c-curve and two dashed line segments for the level-1 c-curve that result from these operations. In effect, the operations produce two shorter line segments that meet at right angles.

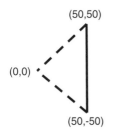

Figure 7.6
A level-0 c-curve (solid) and a level-1 c-curve (dashed).
© 2014 Python Software Foundation.

Here is the pseudocode for the recursive design of the function:

```
Function cCurve(x1, y1, x2, y2, level)
    If level == 0:
        drawLine(x1, y1, x2, y2)
    Else
        xm = (x1 + x2 + y1 - y2) // 2
        ym = (x2 + y1 + y2 - x1) // 2
        cCurve(x1, y1, xm, ym, level - 1)
        cCurve(xm, ym, x2, y2, level - 1)
```

The function drawLine uses the turtle to draw a line between two given endpoints.

Code for the Program

The program includes definitions of the functions cCurve, drawLine, and main. Note that, unlike the mondrian program, the ccurve program draws a line segment as the base case.

```
"""
Program file: ccurve.py

This program prompts the user for the level of
a c-curve and draws a c-curve of that level.
"""

from turtle import *

def drawLine(x1, y1, x2, y2):
    """Draws a line segment between the endpoints."""
    up()
    goto(x1, y1)
    down()
    goto(x2, y2)

def cCurve(x1, y1, x2, y2, level):
    if level == 0:
        drawLine(x1, y1, x2, y2)
    else:
        xm = (x1 + x2 + y1 - y2) // 2
        ym = (x2 + y1 + y2 - x1) // 2
        cCurve(x1, y1, xm, ym, level - 1)
        cCurve(xm, ym, x2, y2, level - 1)

def main():
    # Obtain the level and size from the user.
    level = numinput("Input Dialog", "Enter the level",
                     default = 0, minval = 0)
```

```
   if not level:
       level = 0
   size = numinput("Input Dialog", "Enter the size",
                   default = 100, minval = 100)
   if not size:
       size = 100
   size = size / 2
   hideturtle()
   speed(0)
   pensize(2)

   # Delay drawing if level is greater than 8.
    if level > 8:
       tracer(False)
   cCurve(size, -size, size, size, level)
   # Draw now if level is greater than 8.
           if level > 8:
       update()
if __name__ == "__main__":
    main()
```

You might want to increase the size when the level is greater than 10 so you will be able to see the detail of the lines.

This concludes your introduction to the design of programs with functions. The next chapter explores features of Python that allow you to define new types of data and the operations on them.

SUMMARY

- A recursive solution breaks a problem into smaller problems that are the same form as the original problem.

- A recursive function has two parts: a base case and a recursive step. In the base case, the function solves a problem directly. In the recursive step, the function applies itself, with a recursive call, to a smaller instance of the same problem (in the form of an argument to the function).

- Like loops, recursive functions repeat the same task until a termination condition is reached (the base case). A recursive function uses an if statement rather than a while loop to test for this condition.

- An infinite recursion is an error that occurs when the base case is never reached.

- Recursive functions can be elegant to read but costly to run. When work is done after a recursive call, the runtime system must add memory for each recursive call. A loop-based strategy runs faster and consumes less memory.

- A tail-recursive function, which does no work after a recursive call, can consume the same amount of running time and memory as a loop-based function.

- The sequential search has a linear running time, whereas a binary search has a logarithmic running time.

- Abstract paintings and fractals are examples of structures that have a recursive character.

- The tracer function delays output until the update function is called. However, the computation of the data to be output can continue during this delay.

EXERCISES

Launch the IDLE shell, open a file window, and complete the following exercises. You should run each program within IDLE and, when it is completed, in the terminal window.

1. The factorial of a positive integer, *N*, is defined recursively as follows:

   ```
   factorial(n) = 1, if n == 1
   factorial(n) = n * factorial(n - 1), otherwise.
   ```

   Define and test a recursive function that computes this value. Is this function tail recursive?

2. The Mondrian painting program discussed in this chapter draws randomly colored rectangles. Modify this program so that it fills each rectangle with a random color. Then modify it so that it randomly alternates the positions of the larger and smaller rectangles when it splits a given rectangle in two.

CHAPTER 8

OBJECTS AND CLASSES

Throughout this book, you have been using functions to construct programs that solve interesting problems. Many of these functions, such as the turtle graphics functions and the `math` module functions, are built in to the Python programming language. In Chapter 5, "Defining Functions," you learned how to define your own more specialized functions, and in Chapter 7, "Recursion," you learned how to define functions that can be applied recursively in special situations.

In this chapter, you learn to construct programs that use another important abstraction mechanism. In this style of abstraction, you think of the data and their behavior as the basic program components. Each datum is called an *object*, and each object is of a particular type or *class*. A class specifies the set of *methods* that can be applied to its objects to produce their behavior. But from the perspective of a programmer, objects and classes are software resources like any other. To use these resources, you

- Create objects of a class by running a special function or mentioning these objects as literals (in the case of strings, lists, tuples, and dictionaries).

- Assign these objects to variables or place them in the appropriate data structures (such as lists or dictionaries).

- Get these objects to do things by calling their methods.

- Define new classes of objects if suitable ones do not yet exist.

Now you are ready to explore the use of objects, methods, and classes in turtle graphics.

OBJECTS, METHODS, AND CLASSES IN TURTLE GRAPHICS

When you call a turtle graphics function such as `goto` or `setcolor`, the position or color of the turtle changes. Underneath the hood, turtle graphics maintains a single turtle object that does all this work. Hereafter, this object is called the *system turtle*. Also underneath the hood, other objects represent the window and the canvas on which the turtle does its drawing. If all you need is a single turtle, this arrangement suffices. However, if you would like to use several turtles, you need to be able to create them, give them names or place them in the appropriate data structures, and manipulate them directly by calling methods. In this section, you learn how to do that.

The Turtle Class and Its Methods

The class of all turtle objects is named `Turtle`. This name is capitalized, to distinguish it from the `turtle` module in which it is defined. You can access this class by running the statement `from turtle import Turtle`. At that point, you can create two new turtle objects, named `sleepy` and `happy`, as follows:

```
>>> from turtle import Turtle
>>> sleepy = Turtle(shape = "turtle")
>>> happy = Turtle(shape = "turtle")
```

The new turtle objects have the same default attributes (position, color, heading, and so on) as the system turtle, but they are distinct objects. Most of the built-in turtle graphics functions that you used before can now be called as methods on the new turtle objects. For example, the next session modifies the initial settings of the two turtles and draws some line segments:

```
>>> sleepy.color("blue")
>>> sleepy.goto(70, 70)
>>> happy.color("red")
>>> happy.goto(-70, 70)
```

The only difference between this code and the turtle functions that you have been using thus far is that now you must refer to a particular turtle object when you want it to do something. For example, the following code segment draws a square of length 70 at sleepy's current position:

```
>>> for count in range(4):
        sleepy.forward(70)
        sleepy.left(90)
```

A Random Walk with Several Turtles

You learned about random walks in Chapter 3, "Control Structures: Sequencing, Iteration, and Selection." Now that you can create and manipulate your own turtle objects, you can take several of them for a walk. Figure 8.1 shows four turtles at the end of their walk.

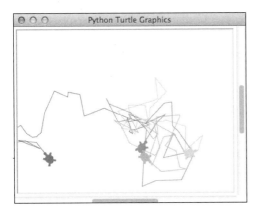

Figure 8.1
A random walk with several turtles.
© 2014 Python Software Foundation.

When you work with many objects of the same type, it's convenient to keep them in a list. In your new random walk program, you create an empty list and then add four new turtle objects to it. Each turtle has a different color (not shown in Figure 8.1). After you add the turtles to the list, you can move them simultaneously by running a loop. On each pass through this loop, a turtle turns left a random number of degrees and moves forward a random distance. The loop through the turtles list is nested within a loop that runs a fixed number of times. Here is the code for the new random walk program:

```
"""
File: randomwalk.py
Four turtles take a random walk.
"""

from turtle import *
from random import randint, random

def randomColor():
    "Returns a random RGB color."
    return (randint(0, 255), randint(0, 255), randint(0, 255))

def main(iterations = 30, numTurtles = 4):
    # Initialize the list of turtles
    turtles = []
```

```
for i in range(numTurtles):
    t = Turtle(shape = "turtle")
    t.color(randomColor())
    turtles.append(t)

# Make them wander around for a fixed number of iterations
for i in range(iterations):
    for t in turtles:
        t.left((random() - .5) * 180)
        t.forward(int((random() - .5) * 100))
if __name__ == "__main__":
    main()
```

Note that the random number of degrees and the distance are generated a bit differently than they were in Chapter 3. For this new program, you use a random distance between –50 and 50. (A negative distance indicates a backward move.) You also use a random number of degrees between –90 and 90. (A negative number of degrees indicates a right turn.) To accomplish this, you use the function `random.random`, which returns a floating-point number from 0 through 1. The expression `((random.random() - .5) * 180` multiplies 180 by a random number between –0.5 and 0.5 to produce a random number between –90 and 90. The expression `int((random.random() - .5) * 100)` produces a random integer between –50 and 50.

Note also that the `main` function allows you to adjust the number of iterations and the number of turtles on different runs of the program.

A New Class: RegularPolygon

Just as you can define new functions when the built-in functions won't do, you can define new classes when the need arises. Classes can represent almost any types of objects you can think of, such as geometric shapes, houses, books, or living things. All you need to think of when you model a type of object with a class is the set of attributes it needs and the behavior it exhibits. In the next two sections, you develop two new classes: a regular polygon class and a menu item class.

You can draw regular polygons rather nicely with the function developed earlier, but you can also think of regular polygons as objects in their own right. They may have other attributes and behavior than their length and their capacity to draw themselves. A regular polygon can be filled or not, can have two colors (a fill and an outline), and can have an area and a perimeter. A regular polygon also has a position and a heading in the turtle graphics coordinate system and can be hidden or shown. Finally, a regular polygon can be *translated* (moved given *x* and *y* distances from its current position), *scaled* (have its size reduced or increased by a given factor), and *rotated* (turned left or right by a given angle). Although you can define functions to represent most of this behavior, it is much more convenient to bundle an object's attributes and behavior in a class. You name this new class RegularPolygon and then begin its design.

Design: Determine the Attributes

You begin by listing the attributes of a regular polygon and their default values (see Table 8.1). The attributes of an object are usually named with nouns (such as length) or adjectives (such as isVisible). The default values are ones these attributes have when a new polygon is created if the programmer creating it does not provide them. Typically, the programmer can override most of these defaults when a polygon is created.

Table 8.1   The Attributes of Regular Polygons

Attribute	Default Value
turtle	A new turtle
length	None; the programmer must provide it
xPos	None; the programmer must provide it
yPos	None; the programmer must provide it
heading	None; the programmer must provide it
sides	3
outlineColor	"black"
fillColor	"black"
fillOn	False
isVisible	True

Note that four of the attributes—the length, the coordinates of the polygon's position, and the heading—have no defaults. This means that the programmer is required to provide her values when a new RegularPolygon object is created. Note also that the attributes include a turtle object, which is used to draw or hide the polygon in the turtle graphics window. The turtle object is created within the regular polygon object when it is created.

Before you consider the behavior of a regular polygon, you'll see how a couple of them might be created. You create a regular polygon by using its class name to call a function. The required arguments are the attributes with no defaults listed in Table 8.1. You can also provide any or all of the other attributes as optional arguments. For clarity, you should use the keyword notation when supplying arguments in this situation. In the next session, you create a square and a hexagon with the given attributes:

```
>>> from regularpolygon import RegularPolygon
>>> square = RegularPolygon(length = 70, xPos = 0, yPos = 0,
                            heading = 45, sides = 4, outlineColor = "blue")
>>> hexagon = RegularPolygon(length = 50, xPos = 80, yPos = 80, sides = 6,
                            heading = 0, outlineColor = "red",
                            fillOn = True)
```

Because the default value of the isVisible attribute is True, both of these polygons appear in the turtle graphics window as soon as they are created.

Design: Determine the Behavior

The behavior of an object consists of the actions it performs when you run its methods. Taking a cue from your experience with a turtle object, two basic behaviors immediately come to mind: showing and hiding the object. Other behaviors relate directly to the polygon object's attributes, such as examining or modifying its colors or changing its fillOn attribute. Behavior also includes what happens when you create a new object. Thus, creating a regular polygon whose isVisible attribute is True immediately draws it in the turtle graphics window. Table 8.2 lists a reasonable set of methods that capture the behavior of RegularPolygon objects.

Table 8.2   The Methods of Regular Polygons

Method	Default Value
show()	Displays the polygon and sets its visibility to True.
hide()	Hides the polygon and sets its visibility to False.
fillOn(value = None)	If value (a Boolean) is provided, resets the fillOn attribute to this value. Returns its current value.
outlineColor(value = None)	If value (a color) is provided, resets the outlineColor attribute to this value and redraws the polygon if it's visible. Returns its current value.

`fillColor(value = None)`	If `value` (a color) is provided, resets the `fillColor` attribute to this value and redraws the polygon if it's visible. Returns its current value.
`isVisible()`	Returns `True` if the polygon is shown, or `False` if it's hidden.
`position()`	Returns a tuple (x, y) representing the coordinates of the current position.
`heading()`	Returns the current heading in degrees.
`translate(xDist, yDist)`	Moves the polygon the given distance and redraws it if it's visible.
`scale(factor)`	Grows or shrinks the polygon by the given factor and redraws it if it's visible.
`rotate(degrees)`	Rotates the polygon by the given degrees and redraws it if it's visible. Positive degrees rotate to the left, and negative degrees rotate to the right.

Note that the methods `fillOn`, `outlineColor`, and `fillColor` work in a similar manner to some of the `turtle` methods. That is, when you supply no argument, the method returns the value of the current setting; when you supply an argument, the method uses it to establish a new setting and redraws the polygon if it's visible.

The next session shows some of these methods in action with a hexagon. The `RegularPolygon` class is located in a new module named `regularpolygon`.

```
>>> from regularpolygon import RegularPolygon
>>> hexagon = RegularPolygon(length = 50, xPos = 80, yPos = 80, sides = 6,
                             outlineColor = "red", fillOn = True)
>>> hexagon.translate(100, 0)      # Move 100 pixels to the right
>>> hexagon.scale(1.5)             # Increase the size by half
>>> hexagon.rotate(45)             # Spin 45 degrees to the left
>>> hexagon.outlineColor()
"red"
>>> hexagon.outlineColor("blue")   # Redraw outline in blue
```

When each of these methods runs, you should see a change in the turtle graphics window, according to the rules of behavior specified in Table 8.2.

Here is a short tester program that displays a radial pattern of 10 hexagons, similar to the one shown in Chapter 3. The program creates 10 `RegularPolygon` objects to do so.

```
"""
testregularpolygon.py
A simple tester program for regular polygons.
"""

from turtle import *
from regularpolygon import RegularPolygon

def main():
    """Draws 10 hexagons in a radial pattern around the origin."""
    reset()
    hideturtle()            # Hide the system turtle
    length = 50
    xPos = 0
    yPos = 0
    sides = 6
    outline = "blue"
    fill = "yellow"
    for heading in range(0, 360, 36):
        RegularPolygon(length, xPos, yPos, heading, sides, outline,
                        fill, fillOn = True)

    return "Done!"

if __name__ == '__main__':
    msg = main()
    print(msg)
    mainloop()
```

Implementation: The Structure of a Class Definition

Each Python class is defined in a module file. Your Python files thus far have contained a `main` function and other supporting functions. Now you are about to define a new Python class, named `RegularPolygon`. By convention, this class goes in a module whose file is named `regularPolygon.py`. To create this file, you open a new Integrated DeveLopment Environment (IDLE) file window by selecting New File from the File menu.

As always, you start the module's text with a docstring that includes the filename and the purpose of the module. You then list any imports for this module. Here is an example for the regularpolygon module:

```
"""
File: regularpolygon.py
Defines a RegularPolygon class.
"""

from turtle import Turtle, bgcolor
```

Note that you do not import all the resources from the turtle module using the statement from turtle import *. Instead, you import only those classes and functions that you need for the module under construction. This tactic helps to prevent errors that might result from calls to functions that you really don't need.

The class definition follows. Its form is

```
class ClassName(ParentClassName):
    methodDefinitions
```

This form is similar to that of a function definition, in which you have a header followed by an indented body of code. But in this case, the indented body of code is a series of method definitions.

Programmer-defined class names are usually capitalized, so you can pick them out from variable and method names. For this class, the ParentClassName in parentheses should be object. Here is the code for the header of the RegularPolygon class and its docstring:

```
class RegularPolygon(object):
    """Represents a regular polygon."""
```

The method definitions are listed one after the other, as you did with function definitions earlier. But note that they must be indented one tab or four spaces to the right of the class header (the line that begins with class).

The form of a method definition is similar to that of a function definition:

```
def methodName(self, otherArguments):
    statements
```

There is one critical difference, however. The first argument in a method definition must always be self. This word refers to the particular object on which the method is called. You then use self to locate this object within the body of the method. Note that self only appears as an argument in a method definition; it is omitted from the argument list when the method is called.

Implementation: The __init__ Method

The first method to define in a class is a special method named __init__. Note the underscores at the beginning and end of this name. This method is responsible for initializing an object's data when the programmer creates that object. Thus, when the programmer makes the call

```
RegularPolygon(length = 50, xPos = 80, yPos = 80, sides = 6,
               outlineColor = "red", fillOn = True)
```

Python automatically runs the method __init__, as defined in the RegularPolygon class. This method assigns any supplied arguments or their defaults to the appropriate data variables within the object and automatically returns a new, initialized regular polygon object to the caller.

The data variables that hold the values of an object's attributes are also called *instance variables*. To pick these out from argument names and temporary variables, instance variable names always begin with the prefix self and by convention use a leading underscore. Otherwise, the code for the __init__ method is much like the code for any function definition that you have seen, although you do not provide a return statement in this method. Here is the code:

```
def __init__(self, length, xPos, yPos, heading, sides = 3,
             outlineColor = "black", fillColor = "black",
             fillOn = False, isVisible = True):
    """Sets the initial state of the polygon."""
    self._turtle = Turtle(visible = False)     # Always hide the turtle
    self._turtle.speed(0)
    self._length = length
    self._xPos = xPos
    self._yPos = yPos
    self._heading = heading
    self._sides = sides
    self._outlineColor = outlineColor
    self._fillColor = fillColor
    self._fillOn = fillOn
    self._isVisible = isVisible
    if isVisible:                   # Display the polygon if it's
        self.show()                 # visible
```

As you can see, when you run the RegularPolygon function, you get a distinct polygon object that contains its own data values; that's what the __init__ method does for each one.

Implementation: Showing and Hiding

The next most important methods are the show and hide methods. These methods display a polygon or hide it in the turtle graphics window. Showing the polygon is straight-forward: you use the code from the regularPolygon function developed earlier, with an adjustment for filling the polygon if its fillOn attribute is True. Hiding the polygon means erasing it from the turtle graphics window. You can accomplish this by drawing the polygon in the window's background color. Each of these methods also adjusts the isVisible attribute to the appropriate value.

Because both the show and hide methods draw the polygon, it is useful to develop an auxiliary method just for drawing. You name this method _draw; the leading underscore indicates that it's a helper method that is not called by other users of this class. Here is the code for this method:

```python
def _draw(self):
    """Draws a regular polygon with the given turtle,
    length and number of sides."""
    interiorAngle = 360 / self._sides
    self._turtle.up()
    self._turtle.setheading(self._heading)
    self._turtle.color(self.outlineColor(), self.fillColor())
    self._turtle.goto(self._xPos, self._yPos)
    self._turtle.down()
    if self.fillOn():
        self._turtle.begin_fill()
    for count in range(self._sides):
        self._turtle.forward(self._length)
        self._turtle.left(interiorAngle)
    if self.fillOn():
        self._turtle.end_fill()
```

Note that you must set the turtle's heading and colors and move it to its position before beginning to draw. The _draw method then checks the polygon's fillOn attribute and, if it's True, calls begin_fill on the turtle object. After the drawing loop finishes, the method checks fillOn again to end the fill if necessary.

The show method is pretty simple by comparison. Here is the code:

```python
def show (self):
    """Displays the polygon."""
    self._draw()
    self._isVisible = True
```

The hide method must set things up so that the _draw method works with an outline color and a fill color that are the same as the current background color (the color of the turtle graphics canvas). This erases the polygon. To accomplish this, the hide method first saves the polygon's outline and fill colors in temporary variables so they can be restored after drawing the polygon (the polygon's actual colors don't change, they're simply hidden). The method then sets both color attributes to the current background color and increases the turtle's pen size before calling _draw. Finally, after the polygon's colors and the turtle's pen size are restored, its isVisible attribute is set to False. Here is the code:

```
def hide(self):
    """Erases the polygon."""
    oldOutline = self.outlineColor()        # Save the current colors
    oldFill = self.fillColor()
    erasingColor = bgcolor()
    self._outlineColor = erasingColor       # Prepare to erase
    self._fillColor = erasingColor
    self._turtle.pensize(3)                 # Make sure outline goes away
    self._draw()
    self._outlineColor = oldOutline         # Restore the current colors
    self._fillColor = oldFill
    self._turtle.pensize(1)
    self._isVisible = False
```

Implementation: Getting and Setting

Three of the polygon methods allow you to either examine or modify an attribute, depending on whether an argument is present. For example, consider the outlineColor method. If this method's argument is not supplied when it is called, its value is None by default. In that case, you just return the current outline color. But if it's not None, the argument is present, and the method should reset the outline color to the new value and redraw the polygon if it's visible. Here is the code for this method:

```
def outlineColor(self, value = None):
    """Getter and setter for the outline color."""
    if value:
        self._outlineColor = value
        if self.isVisible():
            self.show()
    return self._outlineColor
```

The other two methods have a similar structure and are left as exercises for you.

Implementation: Translation, Scaling, and Rotation

Translation moves a polygon a given x distance and y distance. To implement the translate method, you need to hide the polygon if it's visible. You then increment the xPos and yPos attributes by the x and y distances, respectively, and show the polygon if it's visible.

Scaling changes the size of a polygon by a given factor. If that factor is greater than 1, the size increases, and if it's less than 1, the size decreases.

Rotation turns the polygon to the left or the right by a given number of degrees. You assume that a positive number indicates a left turn, whereas a negative number indicates a right turn.

The completion of these methods is left as an exercise for you.

Inheritance: Squares and Hexagons as Subclasses

Suppose you'd like to provide new classes for more specific types of polygons, such as squares and hexagons. With objects and classes, that's easy. Instead of reinventing the wheel and defining whole new classes, you can make the classes Square and Hexagon subclasses of RegularPolygon. In Python, a *subclass* of a given class gets to use the *parent class*'s attributes and methods for free, by *inheritance*. Figure 8.2 shows the relationship between the parent class RegularPolygon and two of its subclasses, Square and Hexagon.

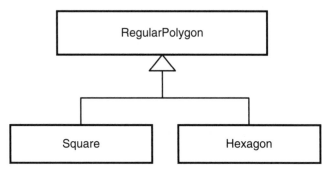

Figure 8.2
A parent class and two of its subclasses.

The only difference between squares and regular polygons, after all, is that squares always have four sides. Thus, to create a new Square object, you call the Square function (but without the number of sides) along with any of the other arguments that you need or may supply for any other type of polygon. Here is an example:

```
square = Square(length = 70, xPos = 0, yPos = 0, heading = 45,
                outlineColor = "blue")
```

The only method that you need to define in the new Square class is __init__, which overrides the default number of sides. Here is the code, followed by an explanation:

```
class Square(RegularPolygon):
    def __init__(self, length, xPos, yPos, heading, outlineColor = "black",
                 fillColor = "black", fillOn = False, isVisible = True):
        # Call the parent's __init__ with 4 sides only
        RegularPolygon.__init__(self, length, xPos, yPos, 4, heading,
                                outlineColor, fillColor, fillOn,
                                isVisible)
```

This code can appear in the same module as the code for RegularPolygon. If this code is in a different module, you have to import RegularPolygon for it to work.

Note that the parent class in parentheses is now RegularPolygon rather than object.

Also note that the method RegularPolygon.__init__ is called, with self as an explicit first argument, within Square's __init__ method. This call of the same method in the parent class takes care of setting all the square's attributes, which already belong to it as a subtype of RegularPolygon.

Because all the other methods are also inherited from the RegularPolygon class, your Square class is ready to be used without further changes! The code for a Hexagon class is similar and is left as an exercise for you.

New Class: Menu Item

Users of graphics-based programs select different commands or other options from menus. Sometimes these selections are offered as drop-downs from a menu bar or as items arranged on a visible palette. For example, suppose the sketching program of Chapter 6, "User Interaction with the Mouse and the Keyboard," allowed you to select a color from a menu of colors. The options could be arranged in a column of colored discs along the left margin of the window. When the user clicks the mouse on a colored disc in this menu, the program would use that color from then on in its drawings. In this section, you develop a new class of menu items to be used in this type of application.

Design: Determine the Attributes and Behavior

A menu item has a position in the window, a shape, a color, and a callback function. A *callback function* is triggered when a user event, such as a mouse click, occurs. You learned in Chapter 6 how to set up the system turtle to respond to mouse click events with the `onclick` function. This function receives a callback function as an argument. From that point on, when the user clicks the mouse within the area of the turtle's shape, its callback function is triggered.

Because all these attributes of a menu item are also attributes of a turtle object, the best way to proceed is to make your new `MenuItem` class a subclass of the `Turtle` class. Then your `MenuItem` class gets all of a turtle's attributes and methods for free.

Because the only thing that a menu item does is respond to a mouse click, you don't have to worry about defining other behavior. All the work gets done when the `MenuItem` object is created. You just provide its position, its shape, its color, and a callback function as arguments to the `MenuItem` function (and also to its __init__ method). Here is an example of a menu item's use:

```
>>> from menuitem import MenuItem
>>> MenuItem(-50, 0, "circle", "red", lambda color: print(color))
```

The second line of code places a red disc at position (–50, 0) in the turtle graphics window and sets its callback function to the `lambda` expression. When the user clicks on the disc, the program prints the disc's color in the Python shell window.

Implementation and Testing

The `MenuItem` class consists of an `import` statement and the definition of the __init__ method. This method expects *x* and *y* coordinates, a shape, a color, and a callback function as arguments. Here is the code for the `MenuItem` class:

```
"""
File: menuitem.py
Defines a class for menu items.
"""

from turtle import Turtle

class MenuItem(Turtle):
    """Represents a menu item."""
```

```
def __init__(self, x, y, shape, color, callBack):
    """Sets the initial state of a menu item."""
    Turtle.__init__(self, shape = shape, visible = False)
    self.speed(0)
    self.up()
    self.goto(x, y)
    self.color(color, color)
    self._callBack = callback
    # Pass my color to the callback function when I'm clicked
    self.onclick(lambda x, y: self._callBack(color))
    self.showturtle()
```

Because MenuItem is a subclass of Turtle, you have to call Turtle's __init__ method first. You can provide the shape and initial visibility as arguments to this method. The turtle is initially hidden, until it's moved to its final location.

Note that self now refers to the menu item under construction, which is also a turtle. So you pick up this menu item by calling self.up(). If you forget to use self and call the system turtle's function up(), you get an error message. Because you imported Turtle rather than * from the turtle module, your code no longer has access to the system turtle's functions. This style of defensive programming helps to prevent logic errors at runtime.

You create a new instance variable for the callback function and call the onclick method to register it. You should pay close attention to the following two lines of code:

```
self._callBack = callback
# Pass my color to the callback function when I'm clicked
self.onclick(lambda x, y: self._callBack(color))
```

Recall that a callback function for a click event is passed the x and y coordinates of the mouse when a mouse click occurs. Therefore, the function passed to the onclick method must be a function of two arguments. But the callback function that the menu item receives from its creator is a function of one argument: a color. So you construct a lambda expression with two arguments to keep onclick happy and hide a call of the callback function with its color argument in the body of this lambda.

Now when the user clicks the mouse on a menu item, its callback function is triggered and passed the mouse coordinates, which are ignored. Instead, the function saved in the instance variable self._callback is called with the menu item's color as an argument. If you go back and look at the code for the callback function that was provided by the creator of the menu item, you see that it has been set up to let the user know which color has been selected.

Here is a short tester program that displays a column of six menu items at the left border of the turtle graphics window (see Figure 8.3).

Figure 8.3
Six menu items (colors not shown).
© 2014 Python Software Foundation.

Note that one callback function is passed to all the menu items when they are created. This time, the callback changes the color of the system turtle when you click a menu item.

```
"""
testmenuitem.py
A simple tester program for menu items.
"""

from turtle import *
from menuitem import MenuItem

def changePenColor(c):
    """Changes the system turtle's color to c."""
    color(c)

def createMenu(callBack):
    """Displays 6 menu items to respond to the given callback function."""
    x = - (window_width() / 2) + 30
    y = 100
    colors = ("red", "green", "blue", "yellow", "black", "purple")
    shape = "circle"
    for color in colors:
        MenuItem(x, y, shape, color, callBack)
        y -= 30
```

```
def main():
    """Creates a menu for selecting colors."""
    reset()
    shape("turtle")
    createMenu(changeColor)
    return "Done!"
if __name__ == '__main__':
    msg = main()
    print(msg)
    mainloop()
```

Response to User Events, Revisited

The presence of multiple turtles presents some interesting opportunities and problems in interactive turtle graphics programs. For example, you might want to allow the user to drag regular polygon objects around in the window after they are created, or you might want to select a polygon for removal. Because a polygon contains a turtle object, it might not be too hard to define onclick and ondrag methods in the RegularPolygon class that have the desired behavior. On the other hand, any program that configures objects to respond to onclick events will have problems when it also tries to respond to onscreenclick events, as does the sketching program discussed in Chapter 6. In this section, you explore how to get different types of objects to respond to user events and how to handle potentially troublesome interactions among these responses.

Whose Click Is It Anyway?

Consider the tester program for menu items presented earlier. This program changes the color of the system turtle when the user clicks on a menu item. Now, suppose you want the system turtle to respond to mouse events as well. For example, the user could drag the system turtle to draw lines, as was shown in Chapter 6. There is no problem here, because the system turtle would be the only object responding to such events in the program. (Recall that the ondrag function targets the system turtle.)

However, suppose you also want to be able to move the system turtle, as you did in Chapter 6, by clicking anywhere in the turtle graphics window. You must use the onscreenclick function to tell the screen to respond to a click event. All will be well, as long as you don't try to select a menu item with a click; the system turtle will move to the click position as desired. However, when you try to select a menu item, the system turtle also moves to the menu item's position!

Here is the code for the relevant functions in the program, so you can see why this happens:

```
def changeColor(c):
    """Changes the pen's color to c."""
    color(c)

def skip(x, y):
    "Moves the pen to the given location without drawing."
    up()
    goto(x, y)
    down()

def main():
    """Creates a menu for selecting colors."""
    reset()
    shape("triangle")
    createMenu(changePenColor)
    onscreenclick(skip)
    listen()
    return "Done!"
```

When you click the mouse on a menu item, the menu item recognizes the click event, as does the screen. Thus, both the changePenColor and skip functions are called. The first function changes the system turtle's color, and the second function moves the turtle to the menu item's position.

Fortunately, the menu item detects the mouse click and calls changeColor first, before the screen detects the mouse click and calls skip. So, if changeColor could inform skip about this fact, skip could simply return and do nothing.

To solve this problem, you can set up a special object, called a *flag*, to track when menu item selections occur. This object contains a Boolean value. The value is True if a menu item selection has occurred, or False otherwise. Your new object belongs to the Flag class, which is defined as follows:

```
"""
File: flag.py
Defines a Flag class.
"""

class Flag(object):
    """Represents a Boolean flag."""
```

```
def __init__(self, value = False):
    """Sets the initial state."""
    self._value = value

def value(self, newValue = None):
    """Getter and setter."""
    if not newValue is None:
        self._value = newValue
    return self._value
```

Now you can add a flag object to your program to enable your changeColor and skip functions to communicate. You initialize the variable, named clickFlag, above the function definitions. Because clickFlag is a module variable, both functions can locate and change the flag. Its value is initially False because no clicks have yet occurred.

When changeColor is called, it sets the value of clickFlag to True. When skip is called shortly thereafter, it sees that the flag's value is True and avoids moving the system turtle. But skip resets the flag's value to False because the next click event might not be on a menu item.

If a click does not occur on a menu item, changeColor is not called. In that case, the flag's value is guaranteed to be False, so skip moves the system turtle to the mouse coordinates.

Here is the revised code that uses the new flag object:

```
from flag import Flag

clickFlag = Flag()              # Create a global flag, initially False

def changeColor(c):
    """Changes the pen's color to c and sets clickFlag to True."""
    clickFlag.value(True)       # Menu item selected, make flag True
    color(c)

def skip(x, y):
    """Moves the pen to the given location without drawing, if a menu
    item has not been clicked. Otherwise, sets clickFlag to False"""
    if not clickFlag.value():   # Menu item not selected, so ok to move
        up()
        goto(x, y)
        down()
    else:                       # Menu item selected, so reset flag to False
        clickFlag.value(False)
```

A GRID CLASS FOR THE GAME OF TIC-TAC-TOE

To play the game of Tic-Tac-Toe, you first draw a 3 by 3 grid of squares. (A napkin or even a flat area on a beach can serve as a writing surface.) You and your opponent then take turns placing Xs and Os on the squares, until the winner lines up three of his letters in a row, column, or diagonal. Figure 8.4 shows a sample outcome of this game in a turtle graphics window.

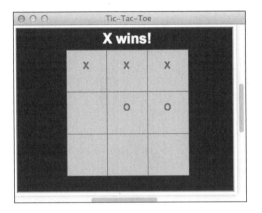

Figure 8.4
A game of Tic-Tac-Toe.
© 2014 Python Software Foundation.

In this section, you develop a grid class and supporting code to play a two-person game of Tic-Tac-Toe. In the exercises, you can then modify the program so that you can play the game against the computer.

Modeling a Grid

A two-dimensional grid is laid out in rows and columns. For example, consider a grid with three rows and three columns, where each position contains an integer. The integers range from 0 through 8. You can easily view this grid in the Python shell by printing consecutive integers in each row, using the following nested loop structure:

```
>>> number = 0
>>> for row in range(3):
        for column in range(3):
            print(number, end = " ")
            number = number + 1
        print()
```

```
0 1 2
3 4 5
6 7 8
>>>
```

If you want to store these data for later use, you can represent the grid with a list structure. The following session places the data in a list and then outputs them in two-
dimensional grid format:

```
>>> grid = list(range(9))
>>> index = 0
>>> for row in range(3):
        for column in range(3):
            print(grid[index], end = " ")
            index = index + 1
        print()


0 1 2
3 4 5
6 7 8
>>>
```

If it seems odd to model a two-dimensional structure with a linear structure like a list, you
can define your own Grid class to represent a grid more directly. You access each datum in
this structure by providing two index values: one for the row and one for the column.
Unlike the coordinate system of turtle graphics, the position (0, 0) locates the datum in
the upper-left corner of this structure. Thus, the datum in row 1, column 2 is at position
(1, 2). The row index gets larger as you move down in the grid, and the column index gets
larger as you move to the right.

The next session assumes that such a class is available in the grid module. You create a
Grid object with the required numbers of rows and columns, and then you can load this
object with data and print its contents:

```
>>> from grid import Grid
>>> datum = 0
>>> gryd = Grid(3, 3)        # Create a 3 by 3 Grid object
>>> for row in range(3):
        for column in range(3):
            gryd[row][column] = datum
            datum = datum + 1
```

```
>>> for row in range(3):
        for column in range(3):
            print(grid[row][column], end = " ")
            index = index + 1
        print()
```

```
0 1 2
3 4 5
6 7 8
>>>
```

In the discussion that follows, you use a list structure to hold a grid's data.

Defining a Class for a Tic-Tac-Toe Grid

Each square in Tic-Tac-Toe is either empty or contains a letter. When a player clicks on an empty square, that player's letter is inserted and displayed there. Thus, a square is complex enough to warrant its own class definition. You call this new class TicTacToeSquare and define it in the module tictactoesquare.py.

When you decide to define a new class, the first question you should ask yourself is, "Can I get some data and behavior for free by subclassing an existing class?" By now, you do not want to write all your code from scratch. You have seen two examples of subclassing in this chapter already: Square is a subclass of RegularPolygon, and MenuItem is a subclass of Turtle. Because you want a Tic-Tac-Toe square to respond to mouse clicks, subclassing the Turtle class looks like a wise move.

In addition to its turtle-like attributes (shape, pen color, fill color, position, and a callback function), a Tic-Tac-Toe square contains two other data values. The first data value is a single-character string. This string will be empty when a square is created and will be either X or O after a player makes a successful move. The second data value is the integer index of the square in the grid. (Remember that you will use a list to contain the squares.) These data are initialized when you create the square.

In addition to the __init__ method, the TicTacToeSquare class includes a text method. This method is the getter and setter for the letter that appears within a grid square. The Tic-Tac-Toe game uses this method to examine the letter within a square and to place a letter in it if it's empty.

Here is the code for the complete definition of the TicTacToeSquare class:

```
"""
File: tictactoesquare.py
Defines the TicTacToeSquare class.
"""

from turtle import Turtle

class TicTacToeSquare(Turtle):
    """Represents a Tic-Tac-Toe square."""

    FONT = ("Arial", 12, "bold")

    def __init__(self, index, grid, length, xPos, yPos,
                 outlineColor = "black", fillColor = "white", text = ""):
        """Sets the initial state of the Tic-Tac-Toe square."""
        Turtle.__init__(self, shape = "square", visible = False)
        self.speed(0)
        self.color(outlineColor, fillColor)
        self.up()
        self.goto(xPos, yPos)
        self.resizemode("user")
        self.shapesize(length / 20, length / 20)
        self._text = text
        self._index = index
        self._grid = grid
        self.onclick(lambda x, y: self._grid.makeMove(self._index))
        self.showturtle()

    def text(self, text = None):
        """Getter and setter for text."""
        if not text is None:
            self._text = text
            self.write(text, align = "center", font = TicTacToeSquare.FONT)
        return self._text
```

Using Class Variables

There is a new type of variable in the TicTacToeSquare class that you have not seen before. The variable FONT is initialized between the class header and the first method definition. This makes it a *class variable*. Unlike an instance variable, which always begins with the prefix self and refers to data that belong to a single object, a class variable refers to data that the entire class of objects shares in common. Because the letters in all the grid squares are displayed with the same font, it is not necessary to keep this font in a separate storage area belonging to each square. That's why you put the font in a class variable, where all the squares can see it and use it. Because class variables usually behave like constants, you spell them in caps.

Note also that the text method, which uses the FONT variable to write the text to the window, must use the class name as a prefix with this variable, as in TicTacToeSquare.FONT.

Stretching the Shape of a Turtle

You decided to subclass the Turtle class rather than the Square class for TicTacToeSquare because grid squares can get more useful behavior from turtles than from squares. However, the turtle's "square" shape is not automatically the same size as your grid square's shape. You don't want the turtle to have to draw a separate square to compensate for that; the square's shape should be exactly the turtle's shape in the window. More importantly, when the user clicks anywhere within the space of a square, the square/turtle should detect and respond to that click.

To get the turtle's shape to be the same size as the length of a square, you have to stretch the size of the turtle's shape with the shapesize method. The two arguments you need in this context are the stretch width and the stretch height factors. For this application, each of these factors should be the length of the square divided by 20. Before running shapesize, you must run resizemode("user").

Making a Move

One of the arguments to the __init__ method of TicTacToeSquare is its grid, and another is its index in that grid. The square needs this information to run the appropriate method when the user clicks in the square. The following three lines of code set up the callback function, which accomplishes this task:

```
self._index = index
self._grid = grid
self.onclick(lambda x, y: self._grid.makeMove(self._index))
```

When the user clicks in this square, the grid's makeMove method is called with the square's index as an argument. From there, it is the grid's responsibility to make the move and update the window.

You can now turn your attention to the grid class.

Defining a Class for the Grid

The grid class is named `TicTacToeGrid`, and it appears in the module `tictactoegrid.py`. This class is responsible for creating the grid squares, laying them out in the window, and managing the game logic. Here is the code for the imports and the class header:

```
"""
File: tictactoegrid.py
Defines the TicTacToeGrid class.
"""

from tictactoesquare import TicTacToeSquare
from turtle import goto, tracer, up, update, write

class TicTacToeGrid(object):
    """Represents a Tic-Tac-Toe grid."""
```

Note that you import just the functions you need from the `turtle` module, not everything.

Laying Out the Grid

The two main attributes of the grid are a list that contains the grid squares and a string that represents the current player's letter. The creator of a grid can specify the size of a square, the position of the grid, the outline and fill colors of the squares, and the current player's letter. As usual, these attributes are initialized in the __init__ method. This method also lays out the squares in the grid. Here is the code for the __init__ method:

```
def __init__(self, length, xPos, yPos,
             outlineColor = "black", fillColor = "white",
             letter = "X"):
    """Sets the initial state of the Tic-Tac-Toe grid."""
    self._letter = letter
    self._grid = list()
    index = 0
    y = yPos
    tracer(False)
    for row in range(3):
        x = xPos
        for column in range(3):
            square = TicTacToeSquare(index, self, length, x, y,
                                     outlineColor, fillColor)
            self._grid.append(square)
            x += length
            index += 1
        y -= length
    update()
    tracer(True)
```

Nothing is unusual here; by now, you should be familiar with the nested loop pattern used to process a grid. The index that identifies each grid square is passed along with self, the grid, to each square as it is created. That information is used in the game logic of the other methods in this class. Note that you call the tracer and update functions to speed up the display of the grid at program start-up.

Defining Methods for the Game Logic

The other methods in the TicTacToeGrid class are concerned with the game logic. The method makeMove, which you passed to each grid square when it was created, is triggered when the user clicks in a square. This method receives the index of the target square as an argument.

The method obtains the square where the click occurred and examines the text contained there. If the text is the empty string, the grid's current letter is put into the square and then set to the other player's letter. The method then checks the grid to see if there is a winner and, if so, announces the outcome. Instead of writing the complex code for checking for a winner here, you pass the buck onto another method, to be defined later. (Remember: passing the buck is a programming virtue.)

Here is the code for the makeMove method:

```
def makeMove(self, index):
    """Responds to a user's click in a square."""
    square = self._grid[index]
    if square.text() == "":
        square.text(self._letter)
        if self._letter == "X":
            self._letter = "O"
        else:
            self._letter = "X"
        winner = self._hasWinner()
        if winner:
            up()
            hideturtle()
            goto(-40, 110)
            write(winner + " wins!", font = ("Arial", 24, "bold"))
```

The _hasWinner method examines the grid and, if there is a winner, returns that player's letter; otherwise, the method returns the empty string. The method must check each row, each column, and each diagonal to see if one of them contains three Xs or three Os.

To do this, the method builds nine 3-character strings from the data in the grid and compares each one to the strings "XXX" or "000", until a match is found or none exists. If a match is found, the corresponding letter is returned; otherwise, the empty string is returned. Here is the code for this method:

```
def _hasWinner(self):
    """Returns the letter of the winner or the empty string
    if there is no winner."""
    row0 = self._getString(0, 1, 2)
    row1 = self._getString(3, 4, 5)
    row2 = self._getString(6, 7, 8)
    col0 = self._getString(0, 3, 6)
    col1 = self._getString(1, 4, 7)
    col2 = self._getString(2, 5, 8)
    dia1 = self._getString(0, 4, 8)
    dia2 = self._getString(6, 4, 2)
    if row0 == "000" or row1 == "000" or row2 == "000" or \
       col0 == "000" or col1 == "000" or col2 == "000" or \
       dia1 == "000" or dia2 == "000":
        return "0"
    elif row0 == "XXX" or row1 == "XXX" or row2 == "XXX" or \
         col0 == "XXX" or col1 == "XXX" or col2 == "XXX" or \
         dia1 == "XXX" or dia2 == "XXX":
        return "X"
    else:
        return ""
```

The method _getString expects the indexes of three squares as arguments. The method builds and returns a three-character string from the text in the squares at those positions.

```
def _getString(self, one, two, three):
    """Builds and returns a string from a row, column,
    or diagonal of the grid."""
    return self._grid[one].text() + self._grid[two].text() + \
           self._grid[three].text()
```

Coding the Main Application Module

The program has one other module, where the main function is defined and called. This module is in the file tictactoeapp.py. The main function hides the system turtle, sets its pen color and the background color, sets the window's title, and creates the grid. Here is the code for this module:

```
"""
File: tictactoeapp.py
A Tic-Tac-Toe application.
"""

from tictactoegrid import TicTacToeGrid
from turtle import bgcolor, hideturtle, mainloop, pencolor, title

def main():
    hideturtle()
    bgcolor("black")
    pencolor("white")
    title("Tic-Tac-Toe")
    TicTacToeGrid(70, -70, 70, "blue", "gray")
    return "Done!"

if __name__ == "__main__":
    msg = main()
    print(msg)
    mainloop()
```

Note that you can make the grid squares larger or smaller, alter the position of the grid in the window, or adjust the colors by supplying different arguments to TicTacToeGrid.

Play on!

SUMMARY

- An object bundles data and operations into a single software component.

- A method is an operation that gets an object to do something.

- A class provides a blueprint for the data contained in a set of objects and the methods they respond to.

- With the exception of the object class, each class is a subclass of another one. Subclasses inherit all data and methods defined in their parent and other ancestor classes.

- The __init__ method is responsible for initializing the data that belong to an object. These data are placed in instance variables.

- An instance variable holds data belonging to an individual object. A class variable holds data available to all objects of that class.

- The Turtle class includes methods that allow you to target individual turtle objects with most of the operations available in turtle graphics.

EXERCISES

Launch the IDLE shell, open a file window, and complete the following exercises. You should run each program within IDLE and, when it is completed, in the terminal window.

1. Complete the code for the RegularPolygon class, and add the methods translate, scale, and rotate. Write a tester program that exercises these methods.

2. Add a menu of colors to the freehand sketching program discussed in Chapter 6. Be sure that mouse clicks on menu items don't cause the system turtle to move.

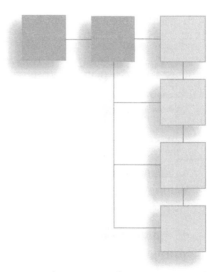

CHAPTER 9

ANIMATIONS

Part of the fun of working with turtle graphics is that you can either move figures around in the window with the mouse or watch them move around on their own. Self-moving figures form the basis of computer *animations*, and these in turn form the basis of video games, cartoons, and animated feature films.

In this closing chapter, you explore some of the features of animations in turtle graphics. After this brief introduction to animations, you will be ready to explore the wider world of computer programming.

ANIMATING THE TURTLE WITH A TIMER

Thus far in this book, your programs have moved the turtle around in the window to draw interesting figures. With the exception of the random walk program, the movement of the turtle has not been a subject of interest in its own right. Indeed, in many cases, you have increased the speed of the turtle to its maximum value so you could focus on the result of its actions, such as a fractal image or an abstract painting.

By contrast, in animations, movement becomes the main point of interest, and coordinating the movements of many objects within a frame becomes the main challenge for the programmer. In this section, you learn to use a timer to start animating a turtle.

Using the ontimer Function

The turtle graphics function `ontimer` calls a function after a delay of time. Here is its form:

```
ontimer(aFunctionOfNoArguments, delayInMilliseconds)
```

For example, suppose you want to move the turtle forward 70 pixels after a delay of 10 seconds and do that twice. Here is how you would accomplish that in a shell session:

```
>>> from turtle import *
>>> reset()
>>> speed(0)
>>> shape("turtle")
>>> ontimer(lambda: forward(70), 10000)
>>> ontimer(lambda: forward(70), 10000)
```

You should notice a slight delay between the moment that you press the Enter key and the beginning of the turtle's movement. Note that you use a `lambda` expression to wrap your function of one argument, `forward(70)`, in a function of no arguments to keep `ontimer` happy. Finally, note that the delay has no effect on the speed of the turtle's movement, once it is initiated; that is governed by the `speed` function, as usual. Thus, other combinations are possible, such as a slow movement after a brief delay.

Now, you might be wondering, "Why bother with a timer at all, when I can already control the speed of the turtle's movements and get some animation with the `speed` function?"

There are three reasons why timers are useful:

1. A timer can schedule actions at regular intervals. You need to do that for animations that run on their own. Using a timer thus enables you to sustain turtle movements for an indefinite amount of time.

2. Using a timer also allows you to control the intervals between actions in a machine-independent manner. Although the speed of the turtle might vary with the speed of your hardware, the interval of the delay that you pass to the `ontimer` function will be the same number of milliseconds, no matter how fast or slow your hardware is.

3. Finally, by introducing a delay into a turtle's sequence of actions, you allow other turtles to perform their actions while a given turtle is "resting" during its delay.

Scheduling Actions at Regular Intervals

You are ready to learn how to use a timer to schedule repeated actions. You will recall the process of drawing a circle described in Chapter 5, "Defining Functions," where the turtle turns left and moves forward by small increments until it completes a circuit. Now you can schedule these actions with a timer.

In the first experiment, you instruct the turtle to turn left and move forward, after a delay of a given number of milliseconds. You then repeat this process, forever. The turtle appears to rotate in a circular pattern (without drawing the circle). To quit the program, you click the mouse in the turtle graphics window.

Here is the code for this program, in the file animate1.py.

```
"""
animate1.py
Animates the turtle using the ontimer function.
"""

from turtle import *

def act():
    """Move forward and turn a bit, forever."""
    left(2)
    forward(2)
    ontimer(act, 1)

def main():
    """Start the timer with the move function.
    The user's click exits the program."""
    reset()
    shape("turtle")
    speed(0)
    up()
    exitonclick()       # Quit the program when the user clicks the mouse
    listen()
    ontimer(act, 1)
    return "Done!"

if __name__ == '__main__':
    msg = main()
    print(msg)
    mainloop()
```

The act function turns the turtle left, moves it forward, and calls ontimer with the act function and a delay of 1 millisecond as arguments. This looks a bit like a recursive function, but it's indirect—ontimer calls act, which calls ontimer again. This recursion is also infinite, because there is no check for a base case condition and no return.

The process starts in the `main` function, where `ontimer` is called with the `act` function and a delay of 1 millisecond and continues forever. Fortunately, before this process starts, the `exitonclick` function is called to let turtle graphics know to quit when the user clicks in the window.

As you can see, the pattern for running code with a timer is a bit like registering a function to handle a mouse or keyboard event. In the case of a timer, the `act` function is the event handler for a single timing event: the tick of the system clock after a given delay. The call of `ontimer` within the `act` function allows the process to go on indefinitely.

The next example uses this pattern to produce a more interesting animation. In this program, the turtle bounces back and forth between the edges of the window until the user clicks the mouse to exit. Here is the code:

```
"""
animate2.py
The turtle turns 180 degrees when it reaches the window edges.
"""
from turtle import *

def act():
    """Bounce back and forth, forever."""
    if window_height() // 2 - 20 <= abs(ycor()) or \
       window_width() // 2 - 20 <= abs(xcor()):
        left(180)
    forward(4)
    ontimer(act, 1)

def main():
    """Start the timer with the move function.
    A user click exits the program."""
    reset()
    shape("turtle")
    speed(0)
    up()
    exitonclick()      # Quit the program when the user clicks the mouse
    listen()
    ontimer(act, 1)
    return "Done!"

if __name__ == '__main__':
    msg = main()
    print(msg)
    mainloop()
```

When you run this program, you can grow or shrink the window's width with your mouse, and the turtle will continue to bounce merrily on its way. Note that the distance of each move is 4, which gives the turtle a fairly quick pace but still allows its movement to appear smooth.

ANIMATING MANY TURTLES

The design pattern just used in animating a turtle works well for the single system turtle, but if you want to animate several turtles, you have to resort to a pattern of objects and classes, as discussed in Chapter 8, "Objects and Classes." In this section, you develop a new class, named AnimatedTurtle, that supports the animation of many turtles at once.

What Is an Animated Turtle?

The AnimatedTurtle class is a subclass of the Turtle class. Thus, an animated turtle has all the features of a regular turtle. In addition, an animated turtle has three attributes that support its animation:

- **Time interval**—This is the number of milliseconds that elapse between each action performed during the animation process. The default value is 1 millisecond.

- **Animated**—This is a Boolean flag that determines whether to pause or continue the turtle's animation. A value of False pauses the animation; a value of True continues it. The default value is True.

- **Callback**—This is a function of one argument. This function is called when the delay on the turtle's timer expires. When called, this function is passed the turtle as its argument. The default value is a function that returns False.

To create an animated turtle, you run the AnimatedTurtle function with the optional/ keyword arguments shown in Table 9.1.

Table 9.1 Optional Initial Arguments for AnimatedTurtle

Keyword	Default Value
shape	"turtle"
xPos	0
yPos	0

(Continued)

Table 9.1   Optional Initial Arguments for AnimatedTurtle (*Continued*)

Keyword	Default Value
heading	0
outlineColor	"black"
fillColor	"black"
timeInterval	1
animated	True
callback	lambda t: False

The behavior of an animated turtle is like that of a regular turtle, because the AnimatedTurtle class inherits all the Turtle methods. In addition, an animated turtle recognizes the methods described in Table 9.2.

Table 9.2   The AnimatedTurtle Methods

Method	What It Does
act()	If the turtle is animated, calls the callback function with the turtle as an argument, and then calls ontimer with the act method and the time interval as arguments.
animated(flag = None)	Setter and getter for the turtle's animated attribute. If flag is absent, the turtle's animated state is returned. Otherwise, flag is either True or False, and this state is reset.
callback(f = None)	Setter and getter for the callback attribute. If f is absent, the current callback function is returned. Otherwise, f is a function of one argument, and the callback attribute is set to this function.
timeInterval(t = None)	Setter and getter for the timeInterval attribute. If t is absent, the current time interval is returned. Otherwise, t is a nonnegative number, and the time interval is reset.

You can examine or change any of the three specific attributes of an animated turtle, even while its animation is in progress. For example, you can increase or decrease the time interval or pause or resume the animation with a shell command. Alternatively, you can access these attributes within the callback function, which takes the turtle as an argument.

Using an Animated Turtle in a Shell Session

In keeping with the practice of trying out new resources in the shell, you can enter a few simple commands to animate a turtle that moves in a circular pattern. You assume that the AnimatedTurtle class is defined in a module named animatedturtle.py, in the current working directory. Then you enter this code in the shell:

```
>>> from animatedturtle import AnimatedTurtle
>>> from turtle import hideturtle, listen, onscreenclick
>>> def moveAndTurn(t):
        t.forward(2)
        t.left(2)

>>> hideturtle()
>>> sleepy = AnimatedTurtle(animated = False, callback = moveAndTurn)
>>> onscreenclick(lambda x, y: sleepy.animated(not sleepy.animated()))
>>> listen()
>>> sleepy.animated(True)
```

When you create this turtle, you set its animated flag to False, so it won't start acting right away. You also pass it a callback function, which turns it and moves it when the animation begins.

You then register a function for screen clicks; this function pauses or resumes the animation. Note the code for this function:

```
lambda x, y: sleepy.animated(not sleepy.animated())
```

The x and y arguments are ignored. The animated method is called twice—first as getter and then as setter—to reset the value of this attribute to its logical negation. This pauses when the animation is underway or resumes when the animation is paused.

Defining the AnimatedTurtle Class

The AnimatedTurtle class is a subclass of the Turtle class. In addition to the turtle's state, this class maintains a time interval and a callback function to be used when the turtle is

animated. A Boolean flag determines whether the animation is currently paused or underway. Here is the code:

```
"""
File: animatedturtle.py
Defines an animated turtle class.
Includes a time interval and a callback function for the timer.
Also includes a Boolean flag to pause or resume the animation.
"""

from turtle import Turtle, ontimer

class AnimatedTurtle(Turtle):
    """Represents an animated turtle."""

    def __init__(self, shape = "turtle", xPos = 0, yPos = 0, heading = 0,
                 outlineColor = "black", fillColor = "black",
                 timeInterval = 1, animated = True,
                 callback = lambda t: False):
        Turtle.__init__(self, shape, visible = False)
        self.speed(0)
        self.color(outlineColor, fillColor)
        self.up()
        self.goto(xPos, yPos)
        self.setheading(heading)
        self._timeInterval = timeInterval
        self._animated = animated
        self._callback = callback
        showturtle()
        self.act()

    def timeInterval(self, t = None):
        """Getter and setter for time interval."""
        if not t is None:
            self._timeInterval = t
        return self._timeInterval

    def animated(self, flag = None):
        """Getter and setter for the animated flag. If set to True,
        starts or resumes the animation."""
        if not flag is None:
            self._animated = flag
            self.act()
        return self._animated
```

```
def callback(self, fun = None):
    """Getter and setter for the callback function. If flag is True,
    also starts or resumes the animation."""
    if not fun is None:
        self._callback = fun
    return self._callback
def act(self):
    """Performs the next callback action if the turtle is animated."""
    if not self.animated():
        return
    self._callback(self)
    ontimer(lambda: self.act(), self._timeInterval)
```

There are two things to note about this code:

The __init__ method calls the act method in its last step because the default state of this type of turtle is to be animated. Thus, by default, the animation begins as soon as the turtle is created.

If the animated state is False, the act method simply returns. This logic allows you to pause or resume the animation by calling the animated method with an argument of False or True, respectively. You can also create a turtle whose animation is initially off by overriding the default value of the animated attribute.

The act method implements the logic of the timer that you saw in earlier examples. In this logic, an action is performed, and then ontimer waits for a given time interval before performing that action again. In AnimatedTurtle.act, the callback function is called with self (the turtle) as an argument. This function can perform whatever actions you want. A call of the act method is then bundled in a function that is passed to ontimer for the next cycle of the animation.

Sleepy and Speedy as Animated Turtles

Your last experiment recasts sleepy and speedy as animated turtles. In this short program, sleepy bounces back and forth in the window, while speedy revolves in a circular pattern. Here is the code for the program:

```
"""
File: animate3.py
Creates two animated turtles. One bounces back and forth, while
the other revolves in a circular pattern.
"""
```

```python
from animatedturtle import AnimatedTurtle
from turtle import hideturtle, listen, mainloop, onscreenclick
from turtle import window_height, window_width
from random import randint

def pauseOrResume(turtles):
    """Pauses or resumes the animation."""
    for t in turtles:
        t.animated(not t.animated())

def rebound(aTurtle):
    """Callback function that fires on each timer event.
    Moves forward until an edge is encountered, then turns
    about face."""
    if window_height() // 2 - 20 <= abs(aTurtle.ycor())or \
        window_width() // 2 - 20 <= abs(aTurtle.xcor()):
            aTurtle.left(180)
    aTurtle.forward(4)

def twirl(aTurtle):
    """Callback function that fires on each timer event.
    Turns and moves forward, as in a circle."""
    aTurtle.left(8)
    aTurtle.forward(8)

def randomColor():
    """Returns a random RGB value."""
    return (randint(0, 255), randint(0, 255), randint(0, 255))

def main():
    hideturtle()
    sleepy = AnimatedTurtle(heading = 0, fillColor = randomColor(),
                            callback = rebound)
    speedy = AnimatedTurtle(heading = 90, fillColor = randomColor(),
                            callback = twirl)
    turtles = (sleepy, speedy)
    onscreenclick(lambda x, y: pauseOrResume(turtles))
    listen()
    return "Done!"

if __name__ == '__main__':
    msg = main()
    print(msg)
    mainloop()
```

The logic of the animation is buried in the two callback functions, rebound and twirl. You saw the logic of both of these types of movement in earlier examples. You can easily change this logic to get the turtles to do other things during the animation.

The pauseOrResume function is triggered on a screen click. The logic in this function is similar to what you saw earlier. In this case, however, the logic is applied to a list of animated turtles.

When you run this program, you should be able to pause or resume the animation by clicking in the window. Be careful to pause before trying to resize the window.

CREATING CUSTOM TURTLE SHAPES

There are several built-in shapes to choose from in turtle graphics, and as you learned in Chapter 2, "Getting Started with Turtle Graphics," you can load a shape from an image file on disk. As you write more sophisticated animations, however, you'll want to create some shapes of your own under program control. In this section, you explore how to create custom shapes in turtle graphics.

Creating Simple Shapes

A quick way to create a simple shape is to get the system turtle to do the work for you. To do so, you use the functions begin_poly, end_poly, and get_poly to create a polygon. These functions are described in Table 9.3.

Table 9.3 Functions to Create a Polygon	
Method	**What It Does**
begin_poly()	Starts to record the turtle's movements.
end_poly()	Ends the recording of the turtle's movements.
get_poly()	Returns a tuple containing the vertices of a polygon created by the turtle's movements.

The first two functions operate much like the functions begin_fill and end_fill do for filling a shape. But instead of filling a shape, begin_poly and end_poly "record" the turtle's movements in a set of vertices, which you can obtain after ending the recording. After calling begin_poly, you run some code that draws a polygon, with the pen up. You then call end_poly to finish the recording. At that point, you can call get_poly to retrieve the set of the vertices. The next session shows these functions in action:

```
>>> from turtle import *
>>> hideturtle()
>>> up()
>>> begin_poly()
>>> for count in range(5):        # Record the vertices of a pentagon
        forward(20)
        left(360 / 5)

>>> end_poly()
>>> get_poly()
((0.00,0.00), (20.00,0.00), (26.18,19.02), (10.00,30.78), (-6.18,19.02), (0.00,0.00))
```

At this point, you can use the set of vertices to register a new shape and then create a turtle with it, as follows:

```
>>> addshape("pentagon", get_poly())
>>> sleepy = Turtle(shape = "pentagon")
```

The result is shown in Figure 9.1.

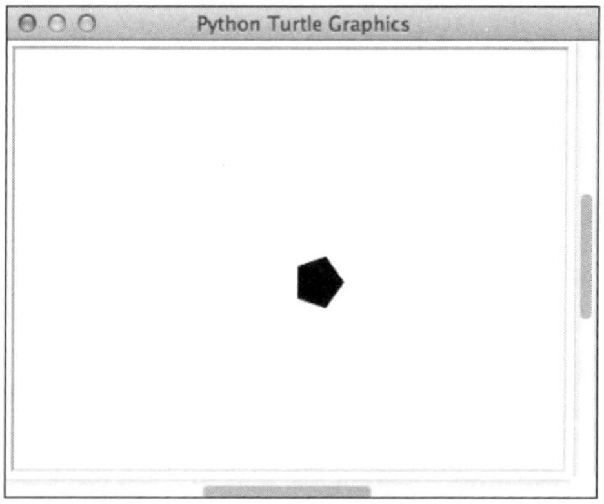

Figure 9.1
Creating a new turtle shape with a polygon.
© 2014 Python Software Foundation.

Note that the pentagon seems a bit off-kilter from the pentagons you drew in Chapters 3 through 5 (the bottom side should be parallel to the *x*-axis). To correct this problem, you can rotate the turtle's shape without altering its heading by calling the tilt method, as follows:

```
>>> sleepy.tilt(90)
```

The next example is a short tester program that defines a function to create shapes that are regular polygons. This function, named makeShape, expects the length, number of sides, and shape name as arguments. It calls the regularPolygon function to draw the shape while recording it, and then it registers the new shape under its name. The main function creates two turtles with different shapes and allows the user to drag them around with the mouse. Here is the code (in the file testpoly.py):

```
"""
testpoly.py
Illustrates the use of begin_poly, end_poly, and get_poly to
create custom turtle shapes.
"""

from turtle import *

def regularPolygon(length, numSides):
    """Draws a regular polygon.
    Arguments: the length and number of sides."""
    interiorAngle = 360 / numSides
    for count in range(numSides):
        forward(length)
        left(interiorAngle)

def makeShape(length, numSides, shapeName):
    """Creates and registers a new turtle shape with the given name.
    The shape is a regular polygon with the given length and number
    of sides.
    Arguments: the length, number of sides, and shape name."""
    up()
    goto(0, 0)
    setheading(0)
    begin_poly()
    regularPolygon(length, numSides)
    end_poly()
    shape = get_poly()
    addshape(shapeName, shape)

def main():
    """Creates two turtles with custom shapes and allows you
    to drag them around the window."""
    hideturtle()
    speed(0)
    makeShape(40, 5, "pentagon")
    makeShape(20, 8, "octagon")
```

```
sleepy = Turtle(shape = "pentagon")
sleepy.color("brown", "green")
sleepy.up()
sleepy.goto(100, 50)
sleepy.tilt(90)
happy = Turtle(shape = "octagon")
happy.color("blue", "pink")
happy.up()
sleepy.ondrag(lambda x, y: sleepy.goto(x, y))
happy.ondrag(lambda x, y: happy.goto(x, y))
listen()
return "Done!"

if __name__ == '__main__':
    msg = main()
    print(msg)
    mainloop()
```

Creating Compound Shapes

Sometimes a simple polygon won't do for a turtle's shape. Consider the shape of even just a simple rocket. It has a rectangular fuselage in the middle, a triangular nose cone at one end, and two tail fins at the other end, as shown in Figure 9.2.

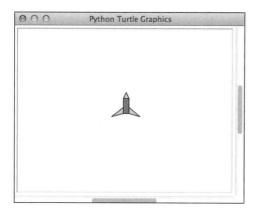

Figure 9.2
A simple rocket shape.

As you can see, this shape consists of a rectangle and three triangles. Python's Shape class allows you to create compound shapes from several polygons. To do so, you obtain a new compound shape object by running the following code:

```
>>> from turtle import *
>>> shape = Shape("compound")
```

You then create representations of the four polygons and add them to the shape, as follows:

```
>>> fuselage = ((0,0), (25, 0), (25, 10), (0, 10))
>>> noseCone = ((25, 0), (35, 5), (25, 10))
>>> fin1 = ((0, 10), (-5, 30), (10, 10))
>>> fin2 = ((0, 0), (-5, -20), (10, 0))
>>> shape.addcomponent(noseCone, "pink", "black")
>>> shape.addcomponent(fuselage, "red", "black")
>>> shape.addcomponent(fin1, "green", "black")
>>> shape.addcomponent(fin2, "green", "black")
```

Note that you can include optional fill and outline colors for each polygon as you add it to the shape.

Finally, you can register the new shape with a name, create a turtle with that shape, and tilt and turn it so it's ready to lift off:

```
>>> addshape("rocket", shape)
>>> Mercury = Turtle(shape = "rocket")
>>> Mercury.tilt(90)
>>> Mercury.left(90)
```

Unfortunately, turtles with compound shapes don't appear to detect mouse events; but other than that, they're good to go!

That's it. Hopefully you have had fun developing your code, viewing the results, and interacting with your Python programs. Now you are a competent Python programmer, ready to move on to the next level. Play on!

SUMMARY

- An animation uses a timer to schedule a sequence of actions at regular intervals.

- The ontimer function takes two arguments: a function of no arguments and a number of milliseconds. The ontimer function sets a timer to run for the given number of milliseconds. When that time expires, the function argument is called.

■ The begin_poly and end_poly functions are used to record the turtle's drawing of a polygon. The get_poly function returns a tuple of the coordinates of the recorded polygon's vertices.

■ The addshape function can be used to register a new turtle shape. This function expects two arguments: a shape name and a shape. The shape can be a GIF filename or a tuple containing the vertices of a polygon.

■ The Shape class is used to create a compound shape from several polygons. The instance method addcomponent expects a tuple of polygon vertices as an argument and adds this information to the shape. You can use a shape object to register a new turtle shape.

Exercises

Launch the IDLE shell, open a file window, and complete the following exercises. You should run each program within IDLE and, when it is completed, in the terminal window.

1. Redo the program in animate3.py so that the two animated turtles do a random walk. Now, you can pause or resume the walk with a mouse click. When a turtle encounters an edge, it should head back into the window on a line perpendicular to that edge. You should incorporate the four specific edge detection functions discussed in Chapter 5.

2. Redo the program in animate3.py to use the shape creation technique to give the turtles the shape of rockets. You should see one rocket moving in a circular pattern and the other rocket rebounding from the edges of the window.

APPENDIX A

TURTLE GRAPHICS COMMANDS

This appendix brings together in one place a reference for the Python turtle graphics commands used in this book, along with a few others. For the commands not listed here, and for the most current documentation on all the features and commands of turtle graphics, visit Python's website at http://docs.python.org/3/library/turtle.html#module-turtle.

TURTLE FUNCTIONS

All the functions listed in this section are functions in the turtle module. Most of them are also methods in the Turtle class. When called as a function, the operation acts on the single system turtle. When called as a method, the operation acts on the turtle object associated with the call. Many of the functions have synonyms; consult Python's documentation for details.

Turtle Motion

The functions in Table A.1 move the turtle and manipulate various aspects of the turtle's state.

Table A.1   Moving and Drawing

Method	What It Does
`backward(distance)`	Moves the turtle the given distance in the opposite direction from its current heading.
`circle(radius, extent = None, steps = None)`	Draws a circle with the given radius. `extent`, if present, is the number of degrees in an arc. `steps`, if present, is the number of steps that the turtle moves to draw the circle.
`clear()`	Deletes the drawings from the canvas. Does not affect the drawings of other turtles.
`forward(distance)`	Moves the turtle the given distance in the direction of its current heading.
`goto(x, y)`	Moves the turtle to the given position.
`home()`	Moves the turtle to position (0, 0).
`left(angle)`	Turns the turtle counterclockwise by the given number of degrees. If `angle` is negative, turns the turtle clockwise.
`reset()`	Deletes the drawings from the canvas, sends the turtle home, and resets its state to the default values.
`right(angle)`	Turns the turtle clockwise by the given number of degrees. If `angle` is negative, turns the turtle counterclockwise.
`setx(x)`	Sets the turtle's x coordinate to `x` and moves the turtle to the new position.
`sety(y)`	Sets the turtle's y coordinate to `y` and moves the turtle to the new position.
`setheading(angle)`	Sets the turtle's heading to `angle` and turns the turtle if necessary.
`speed(speed = None)`	If the argument is absent, returns the turtle's current speed as an integer. Otherwise, the argument can be a number or a string. Speed numbers range from 0 (the fastest setting) through 10 (the slowest). Strings can be `"fastest"`, `"fast"`, `"normal"`, `"slow"`, and `"slowest"`.

`undo()`	Undoes the turtle's most recent action.

`write(arg, move = False,`
`    align = "left",`
`    font = ("Arial", 8, "normal"))`
	Writes the string representation of `arg` to the canvas. `align` specifies the alignment of the string with respect to the turtle's initial position (`"center"` and `"right"` are the other options). `move` specifies whether the turtle moves as a result of writing the string.

The functions in Table A.2 examine the turtle's state.

Table A.2   Examine the Turtle's State

Method	What It Does
`distance(x, y)`	Returns the distance from the turtle's current position to the position (`x, y`).
`heading()`	Returns the turtle's current heading in degrees.
`position()`	Returns a tuple, (`x, y`), that represents the turtle's current position.
`towards(x, y)`	Returns the angle of the line segment running from the turtle's current position to the position (`x, y`).
`xcor()`	Returns the *x* coordinate of the turtle's current position.
`ycor()`	Returns the *y* coordinate of the turtle's current position.

Pen Control

The functions in Table A.3 examine or adjust the state of the turtle's pen.

Table A.3   Pen Placement and Size

Method	What It Does
`down()`	Places the turtle's pen on the canvas, ready to draw.
`isdown()`	Returns `True` if the turtle's pen is down or `False` otherwise.

(Continued)

Table A.3 Pen Placement and Size (*Continued*)

Method	What It Does
pensize(width = None)	If width is absent, returns the turtle's current pen size. Otherwise, resets the pen's size to the given width.
up()	Picks up the turtle's pen from the canvas, to move without drawing.

The functions in Table A.4 examine or adjust the pen color, fill color, and window's background color.

Table A.4 Color

Method	What It Does
color(*args)	Can take zero, one, or two arguments. If there are no arguments, returns a tuple containing the current pen color and fill color. A single argument must be a color value, and both the pen color and the fill color are set to this value. Otherwise, the two arguments must be color values, which are used to set the pen color and the fill color, respectively. Arguments can have the form *colorString* (such as "red" or "#AA0000") or (*r*, *g*, *b*). If RGB values are used, they must be integers in the range from 0 through 255.
colormode(cmode = None)	If the argument is absent, returns the current color mode. Otherwise, sets the color mode to cmode, which must be either 1 or 255. A color mode of 1 allows the use of basic colors only; a color mode of 255 allows the use of RGB values.
fillcolor(*args)	If there are no arguments, returns the turtle's current fill color. Otherwise, resets the turtle's fill color. Arguments can have the form *colorString* (such as "red" or "#AA0000"), (*r*, *g*, *b*), or *r*, *g*, *b*. If RGB values are used, they must be integers in the range from 0 through 255.
pencolor(width = None)	If there are no arguments, returns the turtle's current pen color. Otherwise, resets the turtle's pen color. Arguments can have the form *colorString* (such as "red" or "#AA0000"), (*r*, *g*, *b*), or *r*, *g*, *b*. If RGB values are used, they must be integers in the range from 0 through 255.

The functions in Table A.5 are used to fill shapes.

Table A.5   Filling Shapes

Method	What It Does
begin_fill()	Should be called just before drawing a shape to be filled.
end_fill()	Should be called just after drawing a shape to be filled.
filling()	Returns True if the turtle has started a fill but not ended a fill, or False otherwise.

Turtle State

The functions in Table A.6 examine or modify additional aspects of the turtle's state.

Table A.6   Appearance

Method	What It Does
resizemode(rmode = None)	If the argument is absent, returns the turtle's current resize mode. Otherwise, sets the resize mode to rmode. The resize mode can be "auto", "user", or "noresize". The "auto" mode adapts the size of the turtle to its pen size. The "noresize" mode does not do this. The "user" mode adapts the size of the turtle to the stretch factors and outline width as set by the shapesize function.
shape(name = None)	If the argument is absent, returns the turtle's current shape name. Otherwise, resets the turtle's shape to the shape with this name. The name and shape must be registered in the screen's shape dictionary.
shapesize(stretch_wid = None, stretch_len = None, outline = None)	If the arguments are absent, returns a tuple containing the current shape size factors. Otherwise, resets these factors to the given values, which must be positive numbers.
tilt(angle = None)	If the argument is absent, returns the turtle's tilt angle. Otherwise, rotates the turtle's shape to point in the direction of the given angle. Does not change the turtle's heading.

The functions in Table A.7 are used to show or hide the turtle.

Table A.7   Visibility

Method	What It Does
hideturtle()	Makes the turtle invisible.
isvisible()	Returns True if the turtle is visible, or False otherwise.
showturtle()	Makes the turtle visible.

Event Handling

The functions in Table A.8 register functions that handle events on the turtle.

Table A.8   Functions to Register Event-Handling Functions

Method	What It Does
onclick(fun, btn=1, add=None)	Registers fun as a function to be triggered when the mouse is clicked on the turtle's shape. fun should be a function of two arguments: the x and y coordinates of the mouse click. Optional btn values are 1 (left button) and 2 (right button). When add is True, the existing event-handing functions are not removed.
ondrag(fun, btn=1, add=None)	Registers fun as a function to be triggered when the mouse is dragged on the turtle's shape. fun should be a function of two arguments: the x and y coordinates of the mouse click. Optional btn values are 1 (left button) and 2 (right button). When add is True, the existing event-handing functions are not removed.
onrelease(fun, btn=1, add=None)	Registers fun as a function to be triggered when the mouse button is released on the turtle's shape. fun should be a function of two arguments: the x and y coordinates of the mouse click. Optional btn values are 1 (left button) and 2 (right button). When add is True, the existing event-handing functions are not removed.

FUNCTIONS RELATED TO THE WINDOW AND CANVAS

These functions examine or modify various aspects of the canvas or window.

Window Functions

The functions in Table A.9 examine or modify various attributes of the turtle graphics window.

Table A.9   Functions Related to the Window

Method	What It Does
addshape(name, shape = None)	If shape is absent, name must be the name of a GIF file on disk. Otherwise, shape must be an object of type Shape, or a tuple containing the vertices of a polygon. Registers the shape under the name in the screen's shape dictionary.
bgcolor(*args)	If the argument is absent, returns the canvas's current color. Otherwise, resets the canvas color. Arguments can have the form colorString (such as "red" or "#AA0000"), (r, g, b), or r, g, b. If RGB values are used, they must be integers in the range from 0 through 255.
bgpic(picname = None)	If picname is a filename (must be a GIF file), display the corresponding image as the canvas background. If picname is "nopic", delete the background image, if present. If picname is None, return the filename of the current background image.
exitonclick()	Quits the running program when the user clicks the mouse in the window.
getshapes()	Returns a list of the currently registered shape names.
onscreenclick(fun, btn=1, add=None)	Registers fun as a function to be triggered when the mouse is clicked on the canvas. fun should be a function of two arguments, the x and y coordinates of the mouse click. Optional btn values are 1 (left button) or 2 (right button). When add is True, the existing event-handing functions for screen clicks are not removed.
ontimer(fun, t = 0)	Calls fun after a delay of t milliseconds.

(Continued)

Table A.9   Functions Related to the Window (*Continued*)

Method	What It Does
screensize(canvwidth = None, canvheight = None, bg = None)	If the arguments are absent, returns a tuple containing the current dimensions of the canvas. Otherwise, sets the dimensions and color of the canvas to the given values.
title(titlestring)	Sets the title in the window's title bar to titlestring.
tracer(n = None, delay = None)	If the arguments are absent, returns the current value of n. Otherwise, if n is False, turns turtle animation off until the next update is called. If n is True, resumes animation without calls of update. If n is a positive integer, this specifies that only the *n*th regular screen update is performed. delay specifies a delay of an update in milliseconds.
turtles()	Returns a list of all the currently existing turtles.
update()	Forces a screen update. Should only be used when the tracer is off.
window_height()	Returns the current height of the window.
window_width()	Returns the current width of the window.

Input Functions

The functions in Table A.10 perform text and numeric input.

Table A.10   Input Functions

Method	What It Does
numinput (title, prompt, default = None, minval = None, maxval = None)	Pops up a dialog for numeric input. Returns None if the user cancels, or a floating-point number if the user clicks OK. If default is a number, displays that number in the entry field when the dialog pops up. If minval and/or maxval are numbers, uses them to constrain the input number to a range.
textinput (title, prompt)	Pops up a dialog for string input. Returns None if the user cancels or a string if the user clicks OK.

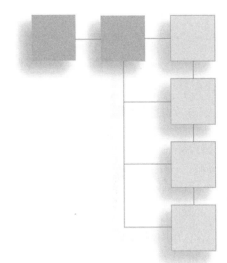

APPENDIX B

Solutions to Exercises

Exercise Solutions for Chapter 1

Exercise 1

```
import math
radius = 45.6
circleArea = math.pi * radius ** 2
sphereSurfaceArea = 4 * circleArea
sphereVolume = 4 / 3 * math.pi * radius ** 3
```

Exercise 2

```
name = "Kenneth Lambert"
name[8:]
```

Exercise Solutions for Chapter 2

Exercise 1

```
from turtle import *
pensize(2)
y = 40
offset = 20
leftX = -60
```

```
rightX = 60
up()
goto(leftX, y)
down()
goto(leftX - offset, y + offset)
up()
goto(leftX - offset, y - offset)
down()
goto(leftX, y)
goto(rightX, y)
goto(rightX + offset, y + offset)
goto(rightX, y)
goto(rightX + offset, y - offset)

y = -40
up()
goto(leftX, y)
down()
goto(leftX + offset, y + offset)
up()
goto(leftX + offset, y - offset)
down()
goto(leftX, y)
goto(rightX, y)
goto(rightX - offset, y + offset)
goto(rightX, y)
goto(rightX - offset, y - offset)
hideturtle()
```

Exercise 2

```
from turtle import *
speed(0)
hideturtle()
length = 40
angle = 90
forward(length)
left(angle)
forward(length)
left(angle)
forward(length)
left(angle)
forward(length)
left(angle)
```

```
length = 50
angle = 72
forward(length)
left(angle)
forward(length)
left(angle)
forward(length)
left(angle)
forward(length)
left(angle)
forward(length)
left(angle)
length = 60
angle = 60
forward(length)
left(angle)
forward(length)
left(angle)
forward(length)
left(angle)
forward(length)
left(angle)
forward(length)
left(angle)
forward(length)
left(angle)
length = 80
angle = 45
forward(length)
left(angle)
forward(length)
left(angle)
forward(length)
left(angle)
forward(length)
left(angle)
forward(length)
left(angle)
forward(length)
left(angle)
forward(length)
left(angle)
forward(length)
left(angle)
```

EXERCISE SOLUTIONS FOR CHAPTER 3

Exercise 1

```
from turtle import *
reset()
speed(0)
for count in range(360):
    forward(1)
    left(1)
```

You can increase the size of the circle by increasing the distance that the turtle moves forward.

Exercise 2

```
from turtle import *
reset()
speed(0)
distance = 1
for count in range(360):
    forward(distance)
    left(4)
    distance = distance + .05
```

EXERCISE SOLUTIONS FOR CHAPTER 4

Exercise 1

```
"""
stopsign.py
Draw a stop sign
"""

from turtle import *

def main():
    reset()
    speed(0)
    hideturtle()
    color("black", "red")
    begin_fill()
    for count in range(6):
```

```
        forward(70)
        left(60)
    end_fill()
    color("white", "white")
    up()
    goto(5, 45)
    write("STOP", font = ("Arial", 24, "bold"))
    return "Done!"

if __name__ == "__main__":
    msg = main()
    print(msg)
    mainloop()
```

Exercise 2

```
"""
samplepattern.py
Draws a pattern using a shape.
Command-line arguments can be number of sides,
outline color, and fill color.
"""

from turtle import *
import sys

def main():
    args = sys.argv
    [numSides, outline, fill] = [6, "blue", "yellow"]       # Default values
    if len(args) == 4:
        [name, numSides, outline, fill] = args              # Sides and both colors
    elif len(args) == 3:
        [name, numSides, outline] = args                    # Sides and outline color
    elif len(args) == 2:
        [name, numSides] = args                             # Just the sides
    numSides = int(numSides)
    reset()
    speed(0)
    pensize(2)
    hideturtle()
    color(outline, fill)
    angle = 360 / numSides
    begin_fill()
    for count in range(10):              # Draw 10 shapes
        for count in range(numSides):    # Draw each shape
```

```
        forward(70)
        left(angle)
    left(36)                        # Rotate them evenly
    end_fill()
    return "Done!"

if __name__ == "__main__":
    msg = main()
    print(msg)
    mainloop()
```

EXERCISE SOLUTIONS FOR CHAPTER 5

Exercise 1

```
"""
pythagoras.py
Compute the hypotenuse of a right triangle.
"""

from math import sqrt

def hypo(side1, side2):
    """Arguments: the two smaller sides of a right triangle.
    Returns: the hypotenuse."""
    sumOfSquares = side1 ** 2 + side2 ** 2
    return sqrt(sumOfSquares)

def main():
    sides = ((2, 3), (3, 4), (5, 6))
    for (side1, side2) in sides:
        hypotenuse = hypo(side1, side2)
        print("Side1:    ", side1)
        print("Side2:     ", side2)
        print("Hypotenuse:", hypotenuse)

if __name__ == "__main__":
    main()
```

Exercise 2

```
"""
testcircle.py
Draws a circle using the regularPolygon function.
"""
```

```
from turtle import *

def regularPolygon(length, numSides):
    """Draws a regular polygon.
    Arguments: the length and number of sides."""
    interiorAngle = 360 / numSides
    for count in range(numSides):
        forward(length)
        left(interiorAngle)

def myCircle(radius):
    """Draws a circle of the given radius."""
    # Using a length of 1, you get a circle of radius 57.5
    regularPolygon(radius / 57.5, 360)

def main():
    """Draw the circle with myCircle in black, then check it
    by drawing the same circle with circle, in red."""
    reset()
    speed(0)
    hideturtle()
    myCircle(100)
    pencolor("red")
    circle(100)
    pencolor("black")
    myCircle(25)
    pencolor("red")
    circle(25)

if __name__ == "__main__":
    msg = main()
    print(msg)
    mainloop()
```

EXERCISE SOLUTIONS FOR CHAPTER 6

Exercise 1

```
"""
samplepattern.py
Draws a pattern using a polygon whose length, number of sides,
pen color, and fill color are inputs obtained from dialogs.
"""

from turtle import *
```

```python
def regularPolygon(length, numSides):
    """Draws a regular polygon.
    Arguments: the length and number of sides."""
    interiorAngle = 360 / numSides
    for count in range(numSides):
        forward(length)
        left(interiorAngle)

def radialPattern(length, numSides):
    """Draws a series of 10 polygons by rotating around a center point.
    Arguments: The length and number of sides of a polygon."""
    for count in range(10):
        regularPolygon(length, numSides)
        left(36)

def main():
    reset()
    speed(0)
    pensize(2)
    hideturtle()

    # Take the inputs via dialogs
    length = int(numinput("Input Dialog", "Enter the length of a side",
                          default = 70, minval = 1))
    numSides = int(numinput("Input Dialog", "Enter the number of sides",
                            default = 3, minval = 1))
    pColor = textinput("Input Dialog", "Enter the pen color")
    fColor = textinput("Input Dialog", "Enter the fill color")

    # Use default pen or fill color if it is not present
    if not pColor:
        pColor = "black"
    if not fColor:
        fColor = "black"
    color(pColor, fColor)

    # Draw the pattern
    begin_fill()
    radialPattern(length, numSides)
    end_fill()
    return "Done!"

if __name__ == "__main__":
    msg = main()
    print(msg)
    mainloop()
```

Exercise 2

```python
"""
drawcircle.py
Draws a circle whose center point is the position of the first mouse click and
whose circumference contains the position of the second mouse click.
"""

from turtle import *

# Used to store the position of the first mouse click.
positionHistory = []

def respondToClick(x, y):
    """Responds to consecutive mouse clicks by using their positions to draw a circle.
    Arguments: the coordinates of the mouse click."""
    if len(positionHistory) == 1:
        # This is the second click, so get the center point from the history,
        # compute the radius, and draw the circle.
        (centerX, centerY) = positionHistory.pop()
        up()
        goto(centerX, centerY)
        radius = distance(x, y)
        setheading(270)
        forward(radius)
        setheading(0)
        down()
        circle(radius)
    else:
        # This is the first click, so save the position.
        positionHistory.append((x, y))

def main():
    reset()
    speed(0)
    pensize(2)
    hideturtle()
    onscreenclick(respondToClick)
    listen()
    return "Done!"

if __name__ == "__main__":
    msg = main()
    print(msg)
    mainloop()
```

EXERCISE SOLUTIONS FOR CHAPTER 7

Exercise 1

```
"""
File: factorial.py
Define and test a recursive factorial function.
"""

def factorial(n):
    """Returns the factorial of n.
    Assumes that n must be >= 1."""
    if n <= 1:
        return 1
    else:
        return n * factorial (n - 1)

def main(upper = 9):
    for n in range(1, upper):
        print("The factorial of", n, "is", factorial(n))

if __name__ == "__main__":
    main()
```

Exercise 2

```
"""
Program file: mondrian.py

Draws an abstract painting after the style of Piet Mondrian.
"""

from turtle import *
from random import randint

def randomColor():
    "Returns a random RGB color."
    return (randint(0, 255), randint(0, 255), randint(0, 255))

def drawRectangle(x1, y1, x2, y2):
    """Draws a rectangle with the given corner points
    using a random color."""
    (red, green, blue) = randomColor()
    pencolor(red, green, blue)
    fillcolor(red, green, blue)
    begin_fill()
```

```
        up()
        goto(x1, y1)
        down()
        goto(x2, y1)
        goto(x2, y2)
        goto(x1, y2)
        goto(x1, y1)
        end_fill()
def mondrian(x1, y1, x2, y2, level):
    """Draws a Mondrian-like painting at the given level."""
    if level > 0:
        drawRectangle(x1, y1, x2, y2)
        vertical = randint(1, 2)
        splitFactor = randint(1, 2)
        if vertical == 1:              # Vertical split
            if splitFactor == 1:       # Do 1/3 and 2/3
                mondrian(x1, y1, (x2 - x1) / 3 + x1, y2,
                         level - 1)
                mondrian((x2 - x1) / 3 + x1, y1, x2, y2,
                         level - 1)
            else:                      # Do 2/3 and 1/3
                mondrian(x1, y1, 2 * (x2 - x1) / 3 + x1, y2,
                         level - 1)
                mondrian(2 * (x2 - x1) / 3 + x1, y1, x2, y2,
                         level - 1)
        elif splitFactor == 1:   # Horizontal split with 1/3 and 2/3
            mondrian(x1, y1, x2, y1 - (y1 - y2) / 3,
                     level - 1)
            mondrian(x1, y1 - (y1 - y2) / 3, x2, y2,
                     level - 1)
        else:                          # Do 2/3 and 1/3
            mondrian(x1, y1, x2, y1 - 2 * (y1 - y2) / 3,
                     level - 1)
            mondrian(x1, y1 - 2 * (y1 - y2) / 3, x2, y2,
                     level - 1)
def main():
    # Obtain the level from the user.
    level = numinput("Input Dialog", "Enter the level",
                     default = 1, minval = 1)
    if not level:
        level = 1
```

```
    paintingWidth = window_width() // 2
    paintingHeight = window_height() // 2
    hideturtle()
    speed(0)
    pensize(2)

    # Delay drawing if level is greater than 6.
    if level > 6:
        tracer(False)
    mondrian(-paintingWidth, paintingHeight,
            paintingWidth, -paintingHeight, level)
    # Draw now if level is greater than 6.
    if level > 6:
        update()
if __name__ == "__main__":
    main()
```

EXERCISE SOLUTIONS FOR CHAPTER 8

Exercise 1

```
"""
File: regularpolygon.py
Defines a RegularPolygon class.
"""

from turtle import Turtle, bgcolor

class RegularPolygon(object):
    """Represents a regular polygon."""

    def __init__(self, length, xPos, yPos, heading, sides = 3,
                outlineColor = "black", fillColor = "black",
                fillOn = False, isVisible = True):
        """Sets the initial state of the polygon."""
        self._turtle = Turtle(visible = False)
        self._turtle.speed(0)
        self._heading = heading
        self._length = length
        self._xPos = xPos
        self._yPos = yPos
        self._sides = sides
        self._outlineColor = outlineColor
```

```python
        self._fillColor = fillColor
        self._fillOn = fillOn
        self._isVisible = isVisible
        if isVisible:                    # Display the polygon if it's
            self.show()                  # visible

    def _draw(self):
        """Draws a regular polygon with the given turtle,
        length and number of sides."""
        interiorAngle = 360 / self._sides
        self._turtle.up()
        self._turtle.setheading(self.heading())
        self._turtle.color(self._outlineColor, self._fillColor)
        self._turtle.goto(self._xPos, self._yPos)
        self._turtle.down()
        if self.fillOn():
            self._turtle.begin_fill()
        for count in range(self._sides):
            self._turtle.forward(self._length)
            self._turtle.left(interiorAngle)
        if self.fillOn():
            self._turtle.end_fill()

    def show (self):
        """Displays the polygon."""
        self._draw()
        self._isVisible = True

    def hide(self):
        """Erases the polygon."""
        oldOutline = self.outlineColor()       # Save the current colors
        oldFill = self.fillColor()
        erasingColor = bgcolor()
        self._outlineColor = erasingColor      # Prepare to erase
        self._fillColor = erasingColor
        self._turtle.width(3)                  # Make sure outline goes away
        self._draw()
        self._outlineColor = oldOutline        # Restore the current colors
        self._fillColor = oldFill
        self._turtle.width(1)
        self._isVisible = False

    def outlineColor(self, value = None):
        """Getter and setter for the outline color."""
        if value:
            self._outlineColor = value
```

```
            if self.isVisible():
                self.show()
        return self._outlineColor
    def fillColor(self, value = None):
        """Getter and setter for the fill color."""
        if value:
            self._fillColor = value
            if self.isVisible():
                self.show()
        return self._fillColor
    def fillOn(self, value = None):
        """Getter and setter for the fill on."""
        if not value is None:
            self._fillOn = value
        return self._fillOn
    def isVisible(self):
        """Getter for visibility."""
        return self._isVisible
    def position(self):
        """Getter for the position."""
        return (self._xPos, self._yPos)
    def heading(self):
        """Getter for the heading."""
        return self._heading
    def translate(self, xDist, yDist):
        """Adjusts the position by the given distances."""
        if self.isVisible():
            self.hide()
        self._xPos += xDist
        self._yPos += yDist
        if self.isVisible:
            self.show()
    def scale(self, factor):
        """Adjusts the size by the given factor."""
        if self.isVisible():
            self.hide()
        self._length *= factor
        if self.isVisible:
            self.show()
```

```
    def rotate(self, angle):
        """Adjusts the heading by the given angle."""
        if self.isVisible():
            self.hide()
        self._heading += angle
        if self.isVisible:
            self.show()
"""

testregularpolygon.py
A simple tester program for regular polygons.
"""

from turtle import *
from regularpolygon import RegularPolygon

def main():
    """Draws a pentagon, translates it, scales it, and rotates it."""
    reset()
    hideturtle()            # Hide the system turtle
    p = RegularPolygon(20, 0, 0, 0, 5)
    p.translate(-50, -50)
    p.scale(2)
    p.rotate(45)

    return "Done!"

if __name__ == '__main__':
    msg = main()
    print(msg)
    mainloop()
```

Exercise 2

```
"""
File: flag.py
Defines a Flag class.
"""

class Flag(object):
    """Represents a Boolean flag."""

    def __init__(self, value = False):
        """Sets the initial state."""
        self._value = value

    def value(self, newValue = None):
        """Getter and setter."""
```

```
        if not newValue is None:
            self._value = newValue
        return self._value
"""
File: menuitem.py
Defines a class for menu items.
"""

from turtle import Turtle

class MenuItem(Turtle):
    """Represents a menu item."""

    def __init__(self, x, y, shape, color, callBack):
        """Sets the initial state of a menu item."""
        Turtle.__init__(self, shape = shape, visible = False)
        self.speed(0)
        self.up()
        self.goto(x, y)
        self.color(color, color)
        self._callBack = callBack
        # Pass my color to the callback function when I'm clicked
        self.onclick(lambda x, y: self._callBack(color))
        self.showturtle()
"""
sketching.py
Simple drawing by dragging the mouse; also allows movement by clicking.
Also allows change of color by click on menu item.
"""

from turtle import *
from flag import Flag

from menuitem import MenuItem

clickFlag = Flag()

def changeColor(c):
    """Changes the system turtle's color to c and sets clickFlag to True."""
    clickFlag.value(True)        #  Menu item selected, make flag True
    color(c)

def createMenu(callBack):
    """Displays 6 menu items to respond to the given callback function."""
    x = - (window_width() / 2) + 30
    y = 100
```

```
        colors = ("red", "green", "blue", "yellow", "black", "purple")
        shape = "circle"
        for color in colors:
            MenuItem(x, y, shape, color, callBack)
            y -= 30

def skip(x, y):
    """Moves the pen to the given location without drawing, if a menu
    item has not been clicked. Otherwise, sets clickFlag to False"""
    if not clickFlag.value():  # Menu item not selected, so ok to move
        up()
        goto(x, y)
        down()
    else:                       # Menu item selected, so reset flag to False
        clickFlag.value(False)

def main():
    createMenu(changeColor)
    shape("circle")
    width(2)
    speed(0)
    pencolor("blue")
    ondrag(goto)
    onscreenclick(skip)
    listen()
    return "Done!"

if __name__ == "__main__":
    msg = main()
    print(msg)
    mainloop()
```

Exercise Solutions for Chapter 9

Exercise 1

```
"""
File: randomwalk.py
Creates two animated turtles for a random walk.
"""

from animatedturtle import AnimatedTurtle
from turtle import hideturtle, listen, mainloop, onscreenclick
from turtle import window_height, window_width
from random import randint, random
```

```python
def pauseOrResume(turtles):
    """Pauses or resumes the animation."""
    for t in turtles:
        t.animated(not t.animated())

def atTopEdge(aTurtle):
    """Returns True if the turtle is at the top edge of the window,
    or False otherwise."""
    return aTurtle.ycor() > window_height() / 2 - 20

def atBottomEdge(aTurtle):
    """Returns True if the turtle is at the bottom edge of the window,
    or False otherwise."""
    return aTurtle.ycor() < -(window_height() / 2) + 20

def atLeftEdge(aTurtle):
    """Returns True if the turtle is at the left edge of the window,
    or False otherwise."""
    return aTurtle.xcor() > window_width() / 2 - 20

def atRightEdge(aTurtle):
    """Returns True if the turtle is at the right edge of the window,
    or False otherwise."""
    return aTurtle.xcor() < -(window_width() / 2) + 20

def rebound(aTurtle):
    """Callback function that fires on each timer event.
    Moves forward until an edge is encountered, then turns
    about face."""
    if atTopEdge(aTurtle):
        aTurtle.setheading(270)
    elif atBottomEdge(aTurtle):
        aTurtle.setheading(90)
    elif atLeftEdge(aTurtle):
        aTurtle.setheading(180)
    elif atRightEdge(aTurtle):
        aTurtle.setheading(0)
    else:
        aTurtle.left((random() - .5) * 180)
    aTurtle.forward(int((random() - .5) * 90))

def randomColor():
    """Returns a random RGB value."""
    return (randint(0, 255), randint(0, 255), randint(0, 255))
```

```
def main():
    hideturtle()
    sleepy = AnimatedTurtle(heading = 90, fillColor = randomColor(),
                            callback = rebound, animated = False)
    sleepy.speed(1)
    speedy = AnimatedTurtle(heading = 90, fillColor = randomColor(),
                            callback = rebound, animated = False)
    sleepy.speed(3)
    turtles = (sleepy, speedy)
    onscreenclick(lambda x, y: pauseOrResume(turtles))
    listen()
    pauseOrResume(turtles)
    return "Done!"

if __name__ == '__main__':
    msg = main()
    print(msg)
    mainloop()
```

Exercise 2

```
"""
File: testrockets.py
Creates two animated turtles. One bounces back and forth, while
the other revolves in a circular pattern.
Each turtle's shape is a rocket.
"""

from animatedturtle import AnimatedTurtle
from turtle import hideturtle, listen, mainloop, onscreenclick
from turtle import register_shape, Shape, window_height, window_width

def makeRocketShape():
    """Creates and registers a new turtle shape for
    a rocket."""
    fuselage = ((0,0), (25, 0), (25, 10), (0, 10))
    noseCone = ((25, 0), (35, 5), (25, 10))
    fin1 = ((0, 10), (-5, 30), (10, 10))
    fin2 = ((0, 0), (-5, -20), (10, 0))
    shape = Shape("compound")
    shape.addcomponent(noseCone, "pink", "black")
    shape.addcomponent(fuselage, "red", "black")
    shape.addcomponent(fin1, "green", "black")
    shape.addcomponent(fin2, "green", "black")
    register_shape("rocket", shape)
```

```python
def pauseOrResume(turtles):
    """Pauses or resumes the animation."""
    for t in turtles:
        t.animated(not t.animated())

def rebound(aTurtle):
    """Callback function that fires on each timer event.
    Moves forward until an edge is encountered, then turns
    about face."""
    if window_height() // 2 - 20 <= abs(aTurtle.ycor()) or \
        window_width() // 2 - 20 <= abs(aTurtle.xcor()):
            aTurtle.left(180)
    aTurtle.forward(4)

def twirl(aTurtle):
    """Callback function that fires on each timer event.
    Turns and moves forward, as in a circle."""
    aTurtle.left(8)
    aTurtle.forward(8)

def main():
    hideturtle()
    makeRocketShape()
    sleepy = AnimatedTurtle(heading = 0, callback = rebound,
                            animated = False, shape = "rocket")
    speedy = AnimatedTurtle(heading = 90, callback = twirl,
                            animated = False, shape = "rocket")
    sleepy.tilt(90)
    speedy.tilt(90)
    turtles = (sleepy, speedy)
    onscreenclick(lambda x, y: pauseOrResume(turtles))
    listen()
    pauseOrResume(turtles)
    return "Done!"

if __name__ == '__main__':
    msg = main()
    print(msg)
    mainloop()
```

INDEX